I've Still Got
Sand
in My
Shoes

Books by Kay Brooks

The Row Series:

Spicer's Challenge
Dreams Fulfilled
Newfound Love

Victory Hill Trilogy:

Northwest to Love
Journey Back to Love

Persistent Intruder
Love Again
Shadows of Déjà vu

Biography

The Dancing Couple

(I've still got)

Sand

in my

Shoes

A Conversation with
Steve Jarrell

Sandi,
Hope you enjoy!
Steve is one 3 a kind!
Kay Brooks

By Kay Brooks

KDB Manuscripts

Front Cover Design by Nicky Seay

I've Still Got Sand in My Shoes

Copyright © 2020
By Kay Brooks

First edition, October 2020
ISBN:9781735427812

All photographs are privately owned by Steve Jarrell
unless otherwise noted.

Published in the United States of America

To: All my favorite Musicians,
You followed your dreams
and your songs sooth my soul ~ Kay

To: Austin Leigh and Stephen Franklin Jr.
Daddy loves you~ Steve

Musicians don't retire;
they stop when there's no more music in them.
~ Louis Armstrong

The true beauty of music is that it connects people.
It carries a message, and we, the musicians,
are the messengers.
~ Roy Ayers

Introduction

Creative people gravitate to creative people. Writers to writers; artists to artists; musicians to musicians. No one else appreciates the driving passion to write, paint or play an instrument. No one else understands the frustration when the muse doesn't flow. We become fast friends, check on each another, offer encouragement when times are tough.

Steve Jarrell was born with a talent for music. He honed the gift, pursued the career, and worked hard to survive the demanding profession. Settled near Nashville, the city of music. In many instances, he was fortunate enough to be in the right place at the right time and became friends with famous people he met along the way. While he followed his passion, he loved his family more.

Someone described him as a walking encyclopedia of music, and I must agree. During the countless hours of interviews and phone conversations, it amazed me all that he knows.

I will admit, I was overwhelmed at first. When Steve talks about music his excitement shows. His eyes sparkle, mouth breaks into a smile and voice fluctuates between smooth descriptions, amusing anecdotes, and moments thick with emotion. Stories intersect and as he talks about his busy life, Steve often gets sidetracked. He likes to sing the tunes his friends are famous for, laughs often about mishaps. He values his friendships and keeping in touch. I often heard "Oh, Steve called me just this morning?"

Kay Brooks

A couple times I found myself staring at my thick binder of notes, wondering *how am I going to do this*? But as I started piecing his life together, the story fell into place and I came to admire the man who followed his passion. No matter where life took him, he always found someone that enjoyed music as much as he did and made the most of each moment.

I spent many hours researching for this book. Rather than just include information, I thought you might enjoy it more if Steve talked about it. Thus, some of the conversations are what he might have said.

Many people helped to make this book a reality. Al Ventura's daughter, Caitlin Ventura allowed us to use her *I've still got sand in my shoes to remind me of where I'm from* tattoo art work on the back cover. Caitlin used to dance to the song on her father's feet whenever she heard the song as a little girl.

Before we begin, I would like to thank Leon Frazier, John Wayne Edwards, Randy Layne, Marshall Pearson, David "Spig" Davis, Nicky Seay, John Faulkner, Billy "Hook" Kain, Barry Sullivan and John Hook for sharing their stories about Steve with me.

Also, Tillie James and Justin Bull for their setup and technical assistance.

And lastly, my husband Wayne who not only travelled with me, listened and interpreted phone interviews, but shared some of his own memories of Steve, and patiently waited for me to close the laptop and fix dinner.

Prologue

Steve Jarrell leaned back in his recliner, folded his hands over his abdomen, crossed his ankles and gave me a broad smile. The light from the floor lamp beside his chair reflected off his silver white hair. Cast a soft glow over his fair complexion and oval face.

We had just toured his office where framed records, albums, posters, and other memorabilia, even a captain's wheel graced the walls. I was drawn to an acrylic painting of a side view of Steve playing his saxophone, a microphone and guitar in the shadows. His white/gray hair, warm complexion, and brass saxophone a poignant contrast to the dark background. A Christmas gift, it had been painted by John Wayne Edwards, a high school friend and fellow musician.

It was Halloween Eve day, 2019, and my husband, Wayne, and I had travelled to Steve's home outside Nashville to hear his story.

The weather was cold – gusty winds caused the temperatures to plummet to the lower thirties before dusk.

I could hear cars on the busy road outside his small bungalow home. As the day progressed, the traffic increased as frantic parents and excited kids began getting ready for their evening of trick-or-treating.

We were spending the brisk fall day inside, reminiscing. Steve in his recliner, Wayne relaxed in another chair across the room and me on the sofa with my preliminary notes and research spread across the cushions.

An area rug covered the wood floor. Flames flickered from the gas logs in the fireplace; chased away the chill, leaving a toasty warmth. Portraits of his parents hung above the fireplace; framed pictures of his son and daughter were arranged on the mantle.

On the wall across from the sofa stood a long floor to ceiling entertainment center filled with the usual TV, DVD player, books and memorabilia.

I had my laptop recording, cup of hot coffee beside me, pen poised over a notepad ready to chronicle Steve's full and busy life.

"You know," Steve's crisp, clear voice began, "I'm a firm believer that God had a plan for me."

He gazed across the room at the artificial palm tree in the corner next to the fireplace.

I followed his look, watched the wind try to whisk the few remaining leaves from the branch of the tree outside the window.

"It hasn't always been easy. But I've led an exciting life, made lots of friends along the way. Without those friends, I wouldn't be what I am today."

Steve focused his brown eyes on me, his mouth curved into a smile.

"We've got a lot to cover," he declared. "Guess I should start at the beginning."

North Carolina

Stephen Franklin Jarrell was born on July 31, 1949, in Winston Salem, North Carolina, the son of Arlon and Mildred Childress Jarrell. He had a younger brother, Stan Jarrell.

"My childhood nickname was 'Rootie'. Billy Kain, a friend of the family, tagged me with that when I was in the seventh grade. He nicknamed everybody in my family. My brother was 'Jake.' Don't ask me where that came from.

"Rootie was derived from Ruther Glen, the place in Caroline County, Virginia, where I often visited my cousin Tommy Jarrell who lived there. I am two days older than Tommy and we've been more like brothers than cousins."

Steve Jarrell was born into a family of musicians.

"My Dad played the guitar. Almost everyone on Dad's side played musical instruments, mostly stringed instruments. They enjoyed bluegrass and mountain music. Not necessarily country music but mountain music.

"In fact, I have a second cousin – Thomas Jefferson 'Tommy' Jarrell (another Tommy) – who is in the history books of the well-known mountain music musicians in the early twentieth century. He played the fiddle and banjo and sang. He received the National Endowment for the Arts' National Heritage Fellowship in 1982 and his first fiddle is in the Smithsonian Institute. I think that's pretty cool," Steve exclaimed with a broad smile.

Kay Brooks

"They also have an annual *Tommy Jarrell Celebration* in Mount Airy, North Carolina," he continued. "It features concerts and dancing, youth competitions, lectures and workshops.

"On Mom's side, my Grandmother Sally Childress and some cousins played guitar. When I stayed with my grandmother, she would often pull out her banjo and we would sing together.

"But not my Mom. Nor my brother. They were more into sports. Stan was four years younger than me and played football."

Music has been the focus of Steve's entire life. In his younger years, he enjoyed listening to family members and their friends play at get-togethers.

"I started off with a toy drum set. Then," he stroked his chin, got a far off look in his eyes, "I can't remember whether it was a class or recreation program, but when I was in the fourth grade, I discovered that little song flute. A tonette. I learned to play some tunes on that. Never had any real training, though, played more by ear.

"Back then, I had more cousins than friends. An uncle was in the radio business and I listened to two radio stations in Winston Salem – WTOB who played top 40's and WAAA.

"The first group I ever remember hearing on the radio was The Coasters."

Steve has a habit of vocalizing lyrics of songs associated with groups whenever he mentions a particular band, so I wasn't surprised when he started snapping his fingers and singing "I've been searchin' (gonna find her), A-a searchin' (gonna find her)."

Steve returned my grin when he realized he'd gotten sidetracked.

"Anyway, WAAA was the third black radio station in the United States and the first black owned station in North Carolina. I loved that station. They had an announcer, Oscar

"Daddy Oh" Alexander and "Daddy Oh" became my best friend.

"I listened to him every night. He played old soul – Otis Redding, James Brown, the Orioles."

Steve paused and smiled as if listening to their melodies.

"Back then, the radio stations also hosted movies in the movie theaters on Saturday mornings. They would have bands perform live on the stage before the movie started. I'll never forget watching Vic and the Versatiles. I was in the third grade, but I decided right there, that was what I was going to do when I grew up."

Steve Jarrell was in the third grade when he realized he wanted to perform in a band. Decided that had to be the coolest life in the world!

He attended Mineral Springs Elementary School in Winston Salem and visited his maternal grandmother in the country just outside Mt. Airy, North Carolina during the summers.

He was introduced to the sounds of Carolina Beach Music from the songs that were played on the jukeboxes at the beach. It was called soul music at that time.

"The summer between third and fourth grades, we went to Grandmother's for what I thought was a vacation, but I ended up living there for the next three years. My parents had decided to separate. Dad had custody but worked in Virginia. Mom worked in Winston Salem and they rotated weekends. Stan and I couldn't leave the state.

"I was nine years old. Back then I read those teen magazines, you know, the ones with the actors and actresses, musicians, and bands in them. I would go upstairs, take a pair of scissors, and cut out the pictures of the musicians, glue them to cardboard and make string puppets. Then I'd decorate a shoe box, so it looked like a stage, turn the radio on and move my string puppets as if they were performing. I'd also stand there in front of the box and hold a broom like I'm singing on a microphone. Sometimes, I turned the desk light on me like a spotlight."

While living with his grandmother, Steve attended Beulah Elementary School in Surry County where he performed on stage for the first time.

"I was in the fourth grade. Played the 'Marine Corps Hymn' on the song flute and was accompanied by Larry Miller on the piano.

"Larry and I would later work together in the '70s and '80s. Larry became the keyboard player for Donna Fargo, The Righteous Brothers and The Judds. He had an auto accident in the later '80s and his injuries prevented him from playing after that."

Beulah Elementary had a school gym where at the age of ten, Steve saw his second live band, The Starlites. And his first saxophone player.

"They wore white suits with plaid lapels and a plaid stripe down the pant leg. They played 'Duke of Earl' and early rock and roll songs, and I just thought that was the coolest thing.

"Their sax player, Caldwell Park, fascinated me. I had spent most of my life listening to stringed instruments and here was a guy whaling on a sax. I had heard a sax on records but never seen a rock n roller play one! I was mesmerized!

"I found out forty years later Caldwell was related to me. A second cousin. I never knew that.

"Up until last year, I did annual benefits in Mt. Airy, North Carolina for the Surry Arts Council in recognition of Jim Lowry. Jim and I played together for many years and once I found out Caldwell was my cousin, I started inviting him to perform at the Blackmon Amphitheatre with me. Caldwell worked for ATF – alcohol, tobacco and firearms – and never performed professionally but played back-up two years before he passed."

"I'm just so glad I was able to work with the guy that made me decide to become a sax player."

Steve, age two.

Steve's first car!

Steve and his parents. Arlon and Mildred Childress Jarrell.

Grandma's House near Mt. Airy, North Carolina.

Grandpa and Grandma Jarrell.

Steve's father, Arlon Jarrell

*Arlon and Alyffe Jarrell,
Steve's father and
stepmother.*

*Thomas Jefferson
"Tommy" Jarrell.
From Surryarts.org.
Photo by David Holt.*

7

Steve's mother with brother Stan's picture in background.

Steve's stepfather, Fred Love

Steve's brother, "Stan" Jarrell.

Steve's Stepsister, Kathi Peregoy

The Star-Lites
The band that introduced Steve to the saxophone. Caldwell Park is second from the left. Steve found out forty years later he was related to Caldwell.

Steve with Larry Miller at a Jim Lowry Benefit in 2008. Steve performed on stage for the first time with Larry Miller in the fourth grade.

Virginia

The summer between sixth and seventh grade Steve and his brother moved to Fredericksburg, Virginia to live with their father.

"Dad owned an ice plant on Princess Anne Street in Fredericksburg and I often worked for him. Sometimes when people comment on my age, I say I'm so old I delivered ice to George Washington."

I smiled because I knew where the story was going.

"Ferry Farm was George Washington's boyhood home and is located a few miles outside Fredericksburg in Stafford County. It is a popular tourist attraction and they had an icehouse which is a large hole in the ground outside the house. My Dad would deliver ice there so the tourists could see how the colonial people kept their food cold. We would stand at the top of a trough that went into the hole and toss three-hundred pounds of ice down into the icehouse. People always laugh when I tell them that story."

Steve started seventh grade at Maury School and wanted to play in the school band, but the band instructor said he didn't have the prerequisite middle school training.

"I was visiting my Mom every other weekend in Winston Salem, and she took me to *Camel's Pawn Shop,* bought me a C-Melody saxophone for sixty dollars. I've got a picture of it around here somewhere. I found an *Easy Steps to Band* book and taught myself to play the sax. Drew the charts and colored in where my fingers needed to be.

"My first performance in Fredericksburg was in a Kiwanis Club talent show at Maury School. I played a snare drum and cymbal behind William Rose who strummed a guitar and sang a Ricky Nelson song.

"I also spent time with another local group, The Saints. Jimmy Adams was the sax player, Billy Hardenburgh on bass, Stuart Jones on drums, Bill McClarence on keyboards, Butch May singer and Key Howard on guitar and band leader.

"I would go over to their rehearsals at Key Howard's house and Jimmy Adams coached me, taught me to play the sax. Butch May taught me microphone techniques.

"In 1962, William Rose was starting a band with Larry Sharpe called The Rebels and this was my very first band. We played every Friday and Saturday night at the American Legion Hall Post #55 for two dollars each. Then the kids started coming to hear us and in six months-time, we received a raise to five dollars each.

"I began as the drummer but when William's twin brother, Willard, learned to play the drums they wanted to hire him. I said, 'Wait! Don't fire me, I will play sax and sing!' They agreed and I was now in my first band!"

At the age of thirteen, Steve's first band was The Rebels

The Fredericksburg Fair was another educational avenue.

Steve laughed. "They had these hoochie-coochie strip shows – two white shows and one African American. The white shows used recorded music for their performers, but the black shows had live music – guitar, bass, drums, and sax. An old guy everyone knew as Grasshopper, would stand outside the tent and be the barker.

"He'd holler, 'if you're under eighteen you wouldn't understand it and over eighty, Lord knows you couldn't stand it.'"

Steve locked eyes with my husband and let out a loud roar. "Remember those days?"

Wayne is one year older than Steve and attended many of the same Fredericksburg Fairs. He smiled but remained silent.

"Anyway, since my Dad owned the Ice Plant, he provided ice to the Fair and Lynwood Samuel would make two trips, one in the morning and then again at night.

"The Fair would be open during the day, but the girls didn't dance. So, the guys in the black bands rolled up the sides of the tents because it was hot and sat back there, jammed music all day.

"I would jump on the ice truck and ride out to the fairgrounds with the morning delivery. I took my sax with me and went over to their tent, learned all the instrumental songs they played. They taught me songs like Alvin Cash and the Crawlers' 'Twine Time' and 'Last Night' by Mar-keys. That was my education.

"All this time The Rebels and I were still playing at the American Legion Post 55 and while I was there, I would get the drums and march in the Drum and Bugle Corp as well.

"My second band was The Infernos, a group out of Spotsylvania County. That's how I met Wayne Mills; he played the bass. Donald Ballard played the drums, Lewis Rowles, and his brother Grayson Rowles played guitars.

"Since I was only thirteen years old, Don had to get permission from my Dad for me to play.

"The Infernos played the Moose Lodge and military service clubs."

Steve chuckled. "Don was responsible for picking me up and having me home by eleven. One time, we were late because the venue had asked us to play an extra hour. When

Don dropped me off at home, my Dad was out looking for me!

"Then I met John Wayne Edwards. He had started a band called The Royals. I loved them because they were older. They also wore these camel hair jackets, so I felt like I was moving up in the music world.

"This is 1963 so I guess I was about 8th grade. The guys were in high school and needed a sax player, so I played with them. Besides John Wayne, there was John Bigelow, George Mann – Chip Reamy after George left – and Leon Frazier who played guitar.

"Leon and I got to be good friends. He was a couple years older and had a car. He would also pick me up and take me places."

My husband and I enjoyed a pleasant visit with John Wayne Edwards, who is also an artist. The interview took place in his art studio. Steep steps led to a second-floor workroom where almost every inch of three walls displayed his work. Additional paintings leaned against one three and four deep along the floor.

"The Royals tried to emulate Robert Williams and the Groovers," John Wayne explained. "They were a very respected band and we looked up to them.

"I needed a sax player and invited Steve to join us. With one stipulation. I told him he had to replace his alto sax with a tenor sax. Steve wanted to be in the band so bad he and his Dad went to *Ross Music Store* in Fredericksburg and bought one. I believe he still plays it. Steve also liked to show it off and would always jump around on the stage."

John Wayne chuckled. "We played at Mandie Hubbard's party and nobody has forgotten it."

I commented that Steve had also mentioned that party and asked what made it so memorable.

"It was a summer night; I think her parents were away from home and we'd been invited to perform there. I think everyone showed up. There were kids everywhere – in the living room, dining room, front yard, back yard you name it."

John Wayne Edwards was a couple grades ahead of Steve in school. When he graduated that Spring and went into the Air Force, The Royals disbanded.

"In the winter of '63," Steve continued his story, "Don Ballard was putting together the X-Citers so after The Royals disbanded, Leon and I decided to go with Don and the X-Citers. Don played drums. Leon played lead guitar. There was also Glenn Nicholls on rhythm guitar, Billy Hardenburgh on bass, Bill Belk played keyboard for a while, and me on sax. When Bill left, they needed someone to replace him, so Bill McClarence and Charles Talley often played keyboard.

"We were a party band and started playing private parties around town as well as college fraternities. Remember, I'm still thirteen years old but we would go to the colleges on Fridays and come back on Sundays."

Steve shook his head and chuckled.

"Glenn Nicholls had a horse trailer that never saw a horse because it became our band trailer. When we performed at the UVA frat parties on Fridays and Saturdays, we would spend the night at the Theta Chi Fraternity house where we played most often. We slept on the couches in the frat house or in the horse trailer.

"Back then, the bands would rent places in Fredericksburg to hold teen dances and charged admission. The X-Citers leased one of the large exhibit halls at the Fredericksburg Fairgrounds. We built a big stage, hung parachutes from the ceiling, added colored lights and called it *The Rainbow Room*. That stage stayed there for several years.

"We also played at the *dragnets.* Those were teen dances held on Friday nights after high school ball games and twice a week in the summers. Tom Faulkner was the pastor at St. George's Episcopal Church from 1946 to 1972. His wife, Mary came up with the name. She worried about the young

15

teenagers going out after the games and said the adults needed to 'take a big net and drag them in.' Thus, the name drag-nets.

"Tom and Mary Faulkner's son, John, was a good friend of mine. He wasn't musically inclined but always liked to be part of our shows and would invariably holler, 'Say John Faulkner' sometime during our performances. I got so I would shout it out to the crowds whenever we performed in Fredericksburg and during one of our shows in later years, he came onto the stage and hollered it!" Steve shook his head. "It got to be a private joke with all my Fredericksburg friends.

"The dragnets were sponsored by St. George's and held in the basement of the church. One night, Phil Heim was playing keyboard, and the loud vibrations of the music caused the light fixture to fall from the ceiling onto the keyboard.

"In the summer, the dances were hot because there was no air conditioning in the church. They would open the windows and I have always remembered those years by the colognes the guys wore. The first year, the whole place reeked of English Leather; the second year, it smelled like Jade East and the third year it was Canoe."

As the crowd grew, the location was changed to the National Guard Armory on Route One.

"My first Virginia Beach performance was at *Seaside Amusement Park* with the X-Citers. Don had a Ford Galaxy convertible and we all wore blue suits.

"One time they set my suitcase aside when they decided to fill the trunk with ice and beer. When we were leaving, they backed over my suitcase. I had tire marks on my suit.
"After the X-citers, I joined The Prophets. Those guys are a whole new chapter!"

This would have been around the time of John F. Kennedy's assassination. I asked Steve if he remembered what he was doing when this happened.

"I think I was in class." Steve looked at Wayne for confirmation. "I remember going to the auditorium.

"Honestly, an event that had a bigger impact on me happened the next year when two police officers – Sergeant Roy Glen Wright and Patrolman William Franklin Mines – were killed behind the Park-N-Shop shopping center in Fredericksburg. The guy that shot them had just been released from prison. "That was my first reality that there was evil in the world."

Steve's first song flute.

Steve's Notes Chart for learning to play the saxophone.

*Steve and his C-Melody
saxophone from Camel's
Pawn Shop*

The Saints.
*Left to right: Key Howard, Jimmy Adams, Stuart Jones and Billy
Hardenburgh. Jimmy Adams coached Steve on playing the sax.*

The Royals.
Left to right, John Wayne Edwards, Steve Jarrell, Chip Reamy, John Bigelow, George Mann and Leon Frazier.

Don Ballard & The X-Citers.
Left to right, Glenn Nicholls, Bill Belk on keyboard, Billy Hardenburgh, Steve Jarrell, Don Ballard and Leon Frazier.

Steve while playing with The Royals with his new tenor sax bought at Bill Ross's Music Store in Fredericksburg.

Steve plays that Ross Music Store saxophone today!

The Prophets

In Spring 1964, Ronny Baker, a James Monroe High School classmate, decided to start The Prophets. I asked where the name came from, but Steve shrugged a shoulder, couldn't recall.

"They had already started when Leon Frazier and I came over from the X-Citers. Ronny played the drums, Danny Dagg was the lead guitarist, and Malone Schooler, the bass. Leon played keyboard and wrote most of the songs that we recorded, I played sax and performed lead vocals.

Ronny's Dad, Roland "Pop" Baker was their manager. He owned *Fredericksburg Shoe Repair*. He was also a self-taught musician who played the fiddle and guitar and sang in the *Gospelight Quartet*.

"Pop Baker was great. He took us everywhere."

The band practiced in the Baker's basement on Fall Hill Avenue. Friends would often come to listen, dance, and socialize.

"We'd start rehearsing early in the afternoon and always stopped in time to climb in the back of Pop's pick-up truck and go to the Fredericksburg Drive-in."

The Prophets' first gig was on the stage at the Victoria Theatre right before the Elvis movie GIRLS, GIRLS, GIRLS.

"We played the Top 40 songs of the day, but also leaned on rhythm and blues and Motown. They didn't call it beach music in those days; it was just called soul music. We did, however idolize Bill Deal and The Rhondels from Virginia Beach. Bill and I became good friends.

"We also played Beatles songs – 'I Want To Hold Your Hand,' 'Hard Day's Night', 'She Loves You' for example. They were great songs and easy to play. One of our classmates, Jim Shellhorse looked a lot like Paul McCartney, and we would always get *Paul* to come up and sing with us."

Steve laughed. "He couldn't sing but he looked good standing up there."

That summer, they performed at Fairview Beach, a small community along the Potomac River in King George, Virginia.

Paul and Edith Floyd owned the *Starlight Pavilion*, a popular gathering place along the water. A pier stretched over the water, marking the boundary with the state of Maryland, where gambling was legal. Slot machines were set up at the end of the pier and older people would gather there to enjoy Glenn Miller and the music of the '40s.

"There were two places to perform at the beach: in the roller rink and down on the pier. We were their house band and played Friday and Saturday nights in the roller rink and on Sundays, we moved down to the open-air deck near the pier. Pretty soon, the *Starlight Pavilion* became a destination stop.

"The Floyds wouldn't let us on the pier in the early days because we were underage, and the pier served alcohol."

Steve chuckled. "Mrs. Floyd monitored everything pretty tightly. Not just the band but the people too. She'd serve drinks on those school-type trays and if she saw a couple slow dancing too closely, she'd smack one of them on the butt to separate them! That's how tough she was!

"We started playing in the summer of '64 and I still go back there at least once a year to perform or for a benefit."

The Prophets also competed in the Fredericksburg Battle of Bands at the Fredericksburg Fair that summer and beat The Saints and The Satellites to win the $250 cash prize.

At that same fair, there was a minor power failure that extinguished the stage lighting and almost cancelled the show. Rescue vehicles aimed their lights towards the arena so the bands could perform.

At another Fair, Steve split his madras pants all the way up the back.

Steve chuckled. "I did the entire show. Just didn't turn my back to the audience.

"We typically played for private functions or after ball games. And dragnets," he added. "We were the reason the location was changed to the National Guard Armory on Route One."

Like the X-Citers, the Prophets performed at college fraternity parties at University of Virginia, University of Richmond, and Hampton Sydney to name a few.

"We were still between fourteen and sixteen years of age," Steve reminded me.

"I was eventually made an honorary Theta Chi brother at UVA because I'd played there since thirteen with the X-Citers, then the Prophets and performed each year with the freshman class to their senior class."

Like the X-Citers, anytime the band played at the fraternity houses, they slept on couches or anywhere they could find a place to relax when not performing.

Two weeks earlier, I interviewed Leon Frazier at the Kingsmill Club near his home in Williamsburg, Virginia.

"I've often wondered if the movie ANIMAL HOUSE was based on our experiences," Leon joked. "Everything that occurred in that movie happened sometime when we performed. Two members of the fraternity had a Jaguar and Lincoln Continental. They were brand new their freshman year and by the fourth year, the Jag didn't have a top and the Lincoln didn't have doors.

"We played at Mary Washington College a lot and I remember parents that lived in *College Heights* would sit outside and listen to us playing. That's how loud we were.

"We didn't just play music," Leon continued. "We put on a show. We quickly realized we couldn't just stand there between songs, so we practiced what to say to segue into the next song. We had a repertoire of songs and every song had a tag on the end of it.

"When we did a James Brown song, Steve would get down on his knees and someone would throw his coat over him. Like what the guy in James Brown's group would do."

Steve laughed when I mentioned this to him.

"One night we were playing in Richmond at a place called *AJ's Gaslight*. It was an upstairs club with the parking lot beneath it. When it came time for the James Brown skit, I was going to run off the stage to an exit door, down the steps, across the parking lot, and up the stairs into the club at the other side of the stage. I had to time it to where I grabbed the mic and fell on my knees at the same time. Well, I forgot that the stage had floor lights and when I jumped up on the stage, my foot landed in the floor light. I tripped, the lights blew up, and there was smoke and all kinds of crashing noises. People were applauding like it was part of the show, but I almost killed myself! Trying to be a showman can be a hazardous job.

"Ronny Baker also liked to show off and would sometimes throw his drum sticks out into the audience.

"You know, The Prophets never drank at any of the dances or frat parties, but it sure taught me how inebriated people acted.

"We didn't do drugs either. Or smoking," Steve added.

The Prophets' circle of fans and friends grew as did the memories. Leon recalled playing in a club at Virginia Beach.

"It was on the water and there were these two beautiful twin girls," he remembered. "We were sitting in the hall playing 'House of the Rising Sun' at three in the morning and the girls heard us. A couple years later, we met them at a frat party, and they remembered us. What's really weird is they were dating brothers."

I mentioned Leon's comment to Steve. He laughed.

"At that time, girls from Mary Washington College did their student teaching at James Monroe High School. A couple times, I would come back to class after a wild weekend playing at the University of Virginia and we would recognize one another from that weekend party. I never said a word about it. I would just smile." The corners of Steve's mouth turned up. "I always got good grades from those student teachers."

I asked Steve if any other memories stood out.

"Once, a couple other guys and I were riding around Fredericksburg and one of the guys that will remain anonymous announced he wanted to buy a case of beer. We did and he proceeded to drink it all. He got totally plastered.

"We were cruising through the *Hot Shoppes* to make the loop and suddenly, our inebriated friend hollered to open the door. Somebody opened the door and he was hanging out, getting sick as we rode around the joint. Everybody was blowing their horns at us.

"He never passed out, but he definitely wasn't feeling good. We decided we couldn't take him home like that, so we went to the car wash on Princess Anne Street and laid him down in the stall. Sprayed him with the water wand to clean him up. Put him back in the car and took him home."

"Another time, we had backed a group called The Clovers. Shortly afterwards, one of the members left the Clovers and formed his own group. He was going to perform at a club in D.C. called *The Bob Inn.*

"I was a senior in high school at the time and wanted to go to D.C. to see the new group. The *Bob Inn* is in the predominately black neighborhood and I invited two guys who will remain anonymous, to go with me. We were walking down the sidewalk and a man said to us, 'you can get killed in this area.'"

"Did you hear that," my friend whispered.

"Just keep walking, don't say anything," I replied.

"A table had been reserved for us up front and when we entered, we realized not only was it all black, but it was a gay transvestite club."

The waitress strolled over and in a very deep voice asked, "can I help you?"

"I had been going to D.C. for years so I wasn't surprised, but I could tell my friends were getting nervous. They started pouring the drinks down and when the band started singing Joe Tex's 'Skinny Legs' a transvestite dressed in red hot pants stepped onto the stage. When he sang 'who will take the girl with the skinny legs?' one of my friends who had had too much to drink, threw his hand in the air and yelled, 'I'll take her!' Well everything stopped. The band quit playing, the place went silent. The lead singer stepped off the stage and escorted us out of the club because he was sure harm would be coming our way if we didn't leave."

Steve laughed out loud, raised his hands palms up. "That's a true story and I'm revealing no names!"

I asked about girlfriends.

"I didn't date much. Never had the time! Didn't even get to enjoy many of the school dances because I was either playing in them or somewhere else just about every weekend.

"And if I had any girlfriends, they wouldn't be around long because they got tired of being band widows, what they called the wives and girlfriends of the band members. They would either stay at home and miss all the events or attend the dances and sit with the other band widows.

"Another very brief memory... I decided to try football. Don't ask me why, I'm not athletic. I can't even catch a frisbee. But I was best friends with Billy Kain and Robert

Chinn and wanted to be like them, so I decided I was going to be a sports guy as well as a musician and tried out."

Steve chuckled. "It wasn't pretty. I got tackled right away. I'm lying there on the ground with this big guy on top of me and dirt in my mouth. I kept thinking about the dragnets and how I could be over at the Armory setting up and getting ready to play.

"And getting paid!"

By the end of 1964, when Steve was fifteen, he was a seasoned veteran and had played in four bands.

Left to right, Steve Jarrell, Ronny Baker, Danny Dagg, Leon Frazier, Malone Schooler.

Victoria Theatre, 1014 Caroline Street.
The Prophets' first gig was performed on the stage there. The
Theater is now an annex to Fredericksburg Baptist Church.

The Prophets performing at a Dragnet at the National Guard Armory in Fredericksburg, VA. Pictures by James Mann for The Free Lance-Star newspaper. October 23, 1965.

They came to dance . . . and dance they did . . . Area teenagers packed the National Guard Armory last night for a post-game party following the Stafford-Orange football game. The Prophets, a local rock 'n' roll band, provided the music—the teen-agers completed the scene.

Staff Photos by James Mann

Arial view of Fairview Beach and the Starlight Pavilion owned by Paul and Edith Floyd. The pier stretched over the water, marking the boundary with the state of Maryland, where gambling was legal.

Tim's II at Fairview Beach today.

New York

In addition to being a popular gathering site for music lovers of all ages, Fairview Beach was a tourist destination with camping and cottages along the Potomac River.

In 1965, Fred Root, from Sidney, New York vacationed there and heard a performance by The Prophets. He invited them to come to New York to perform at the grand opening of a remodeled Teen Center at the Sidney Recreation Center.

He also encouraged them to consider competing in *St. John Terrell's Music Circus*, the World Championship Rock and Roll Band contest in Lambertville, New Jersey.

Steve applied for the band contest and since they were going to the Big Apple, thought they might as well do a few other gigs while there.

One of them being the New York World's Fair where they were invited to perform in the *Tiparillo Band Pavilion*, a large outdoor dance floor and band shell. The Prophets performed in the afternoon and Guy Lombardo and his Royal Canadians played there that night.

"Guy Lombardo was the Fair President Robert Moses' favorite band. The area was supposed to be open, but they added the stage when Guy Lombardo agreed to play six nights a week."

Leon drove his '63 Chevrolet to New York, pulled all their equipment behind in a U-Haul trailer. After playing at the World's Fair, they loaded all their equipment in the trailer and travelled to the Recreation Center in Sidney for their performance that night. For some reason, Ronny Baker wasn't able to play in Sidney and Stuart Jones played the drums.

"We had to park a good way away," Leon stated, "and were supposed to be there at eight but didn't arrive until ten. We were sure no one would be there, but the place was packed. The crowd had waited. Then when it was over, after midnight, they put us up in different houses to sleep."

Because of its size, they had to park the trailer near the top of the parking decks.

Leon shook his head. "I remember having to back the car and trailer up long, steep ramps between cars on either side. I was eighteen years old and thought nothing of it. We didn't think about things like that. We just did it."

Leon wrote many of their songs and during my interview, he recalled sitting in a downtown restaurant and writing "I Still Love You" and "Baby" their first two recordings.

"I would write songs about anything and wrote those two on a legal pad. They were about my first girlfriend who was from Colonial Beach."

While Leon wrote, Steve perused the New York trade papers and found an advertisement offering bands an opportunity to audition in front of producers to hopefully be offered a recording contract.

Steve shook his head. "I called the number and spoke to a man about the ad, quickly realized he was trying to scam us. He said each band had to pay one hundred dollars to play.

"We're trying to audition," I said. "I'm not going to pay you one hundred dollars just to be heard."

"You think you're that good?" the man asked.

"I don't know how good we are," I responded, "but we're good enough to play for free, not pay anybody to listen to us."

"Then come in and play. We'll see how good you are."

"We set up in his office and did Leon's songs. I sang 'I Still Love You' and then played the keyboard so Leon could sing the lead on 'Baby.'

"At the end of the audition, the man made a phone call and shortly afterwards we were introduced to Lee Stone who owned his own independent record label, Stonel Records. He signed us to his label and sent us to Bell Sound where Phil Spector, a big-time record producer did a lot of his work. At that time, Phil was working with the Four Seasons, and a couple other well-known groups.

The Prophets recorded "Baby" and "I Still Love You" then travelled to Lambertville, New Jersey to participate in *St. John Terrell's Music Circus,* otherwise known as the *World Rock n Roll Championship.*

The Music Circus was founded in 1949 by St. John "Sinjin" Terrell, an actor who served in the Philippines with the USO during World War II.

It originally featured Broadway theatrical productions in a summer stock setting in the middle of a large field on Route 202. Two thousand sloping seats surrounded a large wooden stage under a circus tent. A tunnel off a back side of the stage led to underground dressing rooms beneath the audience.

The theme was expanded to music – jazz to rock and roll – in the '60s and from 1965 to 1968, bands from across the country competed. First prize was $1,000, a recording contract and a TV appearance.

The contest began with 900 bands from all over the U.S., Mexico, and Canada. It ran all summer long and was eventually narrowed down to where The Prophets were one of the final six bands.

Steve and Leon both remembered the revolving stage, circus tent, and lots of cameras filming the event. It was hot as people stood around, or nervously wandered between the parked cars that lined the outskirts of the field while waiting for their turn on the stage.

"There was a robotic stage with three bands at a time," Steve explained. "We had to perform two original songs – a slow song then a fast one. We decided to do 'I Still Love You' and 'Baby.'

"One of the judging questions was 'If you were on TV and the sound went off, would your physical appearance still attract the viewer and keep him or her from changing the channel?'

"We knew most of the acts were dressing 'mod' because of the Beatles invasion, so we decided to be different. Being *The Prophets*, someone came up with the toga and sandals idea. I can't remember who.

"Ronny's mother made our first togas from sheets and since Pop owned a shoe repair shop, he made our sandals. We were dressed in Roman looking sandals with thongs that crisscrossed to our knees, flowing white togas with blue sashes and garlands or wreaths on our heads.

"Bruce Morrow, better known as *Cousin Brucie* a radio announcer, Pulitzer Prize winner James A. Michener, record producer Phil Spector, and Miss Teenage America were the judges.

"I remember Cousin Brucie arriving by helicopter and waving to everyone as he walked across the field. And James Michener mentioned us in his New York Times article 'One Near Square Who Doesn't Knock the Rock.' He also included a picture of us on the stage."

The Prophets won third place.

"The Galaxies IV were the local band and they won mainly because they had one hundred people in the audience. We didn't have a chance.

"It was a fun time, though. I remember the other acts laughing at our outfits, but," he shrugged a shoulder, "it worked for us.

"We released 'I Still Love You' after the competition and it became a regional hit in 1965.

"Fast forward to 1984, 'I Still Love You' was included on an album – Signed, D.C. – a compilation of songs by 'garage bands' in the District of Columbia area.

The Prophets was Steve's first recording group and they scored three regional hits in 1965 and 1966. Their first record - started at Fairview Beach.

Top to bottom, Danny Dagg, Steve Jarrell, Leon Frazier, Malone Schooler, Ronny Baker.

St. John Terrell's
MUSIC CIRCUS
Lambertville, New Jersey

August 31, 1965

Dear Winner:

Since you appeared here at the Music Circus, we have been negotiating with a major television and radio network and at this time there appears to be a good possibility that a program will be developed. If this interests you and you are free to accept a television contract, then please sign the enclosed forms.

Cordially,

St. John Terrell

SJT:es
Enclosures

St. John Terrell's Music Circus television and radio proposal.

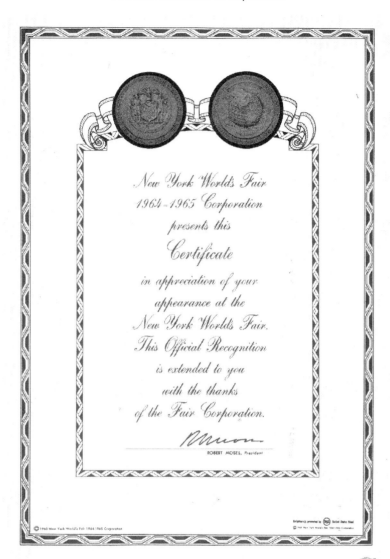

Certificate of Appreciation for performing at the New York World's Fair.

Stardom

The Prophets might not have won the *World Championship Rock and Roll Contest*, but their name was out there. The band promoted their songs whenever they could.

Pop Baker remained their manager and they became one of three bands that dominated the local scene for young people in the '60s. They played as far north as Sidney, New York and south as North Carolina.

The Prophets continued to perform at Fairview Beach, wherever requested and had charge accounts at clothing stores and restaurants.

"We would charge during the week and go around on Mondays and pay our tabs after we worked the weekends," Steve explained.

"This was probably about the time I got my first car. Leon and Billy Kain were crazy about cars and Billy painted them. I had bought this tan car but wanted it to be canary yellow. Billy and I got the paint but ran out, so we had to add some other to it and the car ended up being school bus orange."

Billy Kain had already told me the story of his '49 Ford he had painted gray.

"After I painted it, a bunch of us were cruising around in it one Saturday morning and we noticed an armored car at the Park-N-Shop. We parked up the hill and watched them load and unload the money. This was back in the '60s and we'd never observed an actual stop. The guard came out, threw the bag inside, then saw us watching them. He immediately jumped inside the truck and they sat watching us!

"We never got out of the car but figured we must have spooked them, so we left. We even went to the police station in Fredericksburg to explain what had happened. 'Yeah, they said, we heard all about it and were getting ready to send someone to look for a suspicious gray car.'"

Steve laughed when I mentioned Billy's comments. "We just wanted to watch the transfer!

"Life was pretty cool at that time; we were basking in our success. Then somebody said we needed to do a protest song, since the Vietnam War was so unpopular. Barry McGuire's 'Eve of Destruction' was the number one song at the time."

Leon was a Senior at James Monroe and facing the draft any day after graduation. He was also dating the girl who would become his first wife, and fantasized being drafted and going to Nam.

"I wrote 'Fightin' For Sam' in about fifteen minutes. If you listen to the lyrics – 'I can't go back cause I've got to stay and fight. Yes, I'm fightin' for Sam, I've got to free this land; I've got to give him a hand' – it turned out to be more an anti-protest song. Supported the military overseas which was rare during a time of protest."

In 1966, Billy Arnold and Joel Bragg produced "Fightin' For Sam" and an instrumental of "Misty" in the Bell Studios and released the 45 RPM record on the Stonel Label.

"Fightin' For Sam" made the Billboard charts and received a *B+* rating in *Billboard* magazine.

During his interview, Leon touched on how school life changed for them.

"We had to maintain an image and as we got into making the records, we had to get the record company to write a letter to the school saying we needed to leave our hair long. We also needed permission to be away from school for promotional events. James Monroe High School gave their approval and for the most part, things went smoothly.

"Until Ronny Baker bleached his long hair. The Principal, Howard O. Sullins, called Ronny into his office and kicked him out of school." Leon chuckled. "It made the front page of the *National Enquirer,* 'Principal Expels Kid From School.'"

Leon has always enjoyed cars – "I've owned sixty-three in my lifetime" – and in addition to playing in the band, he worked nights to support that passion.

"I remember one day, my English teacher asked why I always slept in his class. I pointed out the window, to the brand-new black Chevrolet parked next to the light pole in the parking lot. 'That's why,' I responded. 'That's mine.'"

The Prophets were the only white act on an African American label in New York and often travelled there to promote their records.

"One time, we rode down Broadway to a teen magazine interview at *Sardi's Restaurant* in a white chariot pulled by two white horses. We were dressed in our Togas," Steve bragged.

Cousin Brucie invited them to perform at *Palisades Park* where they were the opening act for Dionne Warwick.

In one week, they performed in Washington, D.C. on the *Bob King TV Show,* a dance show like *American Bandstand* that came on 4:00 – 5:00 PM on WDCA Channel 20. Bill Miller, TV and radio broadcaster was the host.

The next day, Thursday, they were in New York performing on the *Clay Cole Show* with the Bobby Fuller Four. Clay Cole was an American host and disk jockey who started at *Palisades Amusement Park* in New Jersey but moved to WNTA-TV and WPIX-TV in New York. The TV show staged a full one-hour long Motown Special that was said to be quite groundbreaking at the time.

On Friday, they played on the radio station WMCA's *Good Guys Show* with Harry Harrison and Jack Spector in James Madison High School in Brooklyn with Brian Hyland.

"I remember being in awe of Brian," Steve said. "He was there promoting his songs and we were there for the Prophets. We performed for free, but it was a way of getting your name out there."

The Prophets also appeared at the National Press Club in DC.

"We even performed in the Metropole Lounge, a famous private social club in Manhattan where the world-famous drummer, Gene Krupa played at night. We performed there one afternoon, behind the bar, but never again because we were underage. I remember there was a policeman out front telling everyone to 'keep moving.'"

"One of the highlights for me was meeting Jackie Wilson in front of Macy's Department Store. It was snowing and cold and Jackie gave us a ride back to our hotel in his limo! I would later meet him again at UVA. That's another story.

"Georgia Nicholas with the Nicholas Literary Agency had approached us at St. John Terrell's Music Circus about doing a movie. Leon has the script. Nothing really came of it though. We often wondered if the movie BOYS IN THE BAND might have been based on us."

They were also offered an opportunity to perform in a weekly TV show, but the show never materialized.

The Prophets thought they were on the road to stardom and Leon remembered bragging to his father.

"Here we were in high school, had made a couple records, gone to New York, and done a TV show. We thought we had made it. Then the guy went bankrupt."

When Stonel Records folded, Steve and Leon went to Imperial Records to see if they would promote "Fightin' for Sam."

"They said, 'we heard it and we like it but because you are still under contract with Stonel, Imperial can do nothing with it."

"Fightin' For Sam" would later be included on an album in England called The Last Generation II.

"They were the best years of my life. Personnel wise, the Prophets was the best band I was ever involved in. We all remained friends and would get together each year."

The Prophets
Top to bottom, Danny Dagg, Malone Schooler, Leon Frazier, Ronny Baker and Steve Jarrell.

r, Fredericksburg, Virginia
August 27, 1965

ROCKIN' ROMANS–Ancient Romans may or may not have looked like these five local teen-agers who compose "The Prophets" musical combo. They say the garb attracts attention and helped earn them a finalist spot in a nationwide band contest. From left are Ronnie Baker, Danny Dagg, Malone Schooler, Leon Frazier and Steve Jarrell. (Staff Photo by John C. Goolrick)

From the Fredericksburg Free Lance-Star, August 27, 1965.

THE PROPHETS - 1964-67

Fightin' for Sam was more an anti-protest song.
It was later released on an album, the Last Generation II.

In 1984, "I Still Love You" was included on an album, Signed D.C.,
a compilation of songs by "garage bands" in the District of
Columbia area.

Reunions

The Prophets' final recording was made in 1978 on their own label, Reunion Records, at the band's ten-year reunion. Two of Leon Frazier songs, "Looking At You From A Distance" and "Feelings Are Just Memories" were recorded in Richmond, Virginia at the Alpha Audio Studio.

"We hired two women, Janice Sealy and Diane Appelin, to accompany us and I think that record is our best," Leon told me.

He wrote "Feelings Are Just Memories" when he managed a hotel in Richmond.

"A lady who worked for me had just had an argument with her boyfriend in the lobby. I went upstairs and wrote the song on the hotel piano. My words were, 'she can't understand, she doesn't know why.'

"Steve had just broken up with his girlfriend and he changed it to 'I can't understand, I just don't know why.'"

The Prophets' last appearance with all five original members was on September 27, 1986 at a twenty-year reunion for the "Music Under the Stars" series in the courtyard at Merchants Plaza in Fredericksburg, Virginia.

It was sponsored by the Fredericksburg Central Association downtown merchants. Twelve other bluegrass, gospel and country bands participated but The Prophets were the main attraction.

"Pop" Baker was one of the sponsors and the event was promoted as the *Grand Finale* featuring music and prizes all day.

The first generation – Steve, Leon, Malone, Ronny and Danny – performed their five hits then the second generation – Rob Spratt, Tom Waite, Gary Ferguson, Henry Marsh, Cary Leitch, Phil Harding and Bernie Mason closed the evening.

1986 ~ Twenty Year Reunion

Poster advertisement for the 20-year reunion "Music Under the Stars" in the Merchants Plaza in Fredericksburg, Virginia.

"Ronny" (Ronald E.) Baker continued to play locally in Fredericksburg while keeping his father's shoe repair business open. He died on June 30, 2017.

Ronny Baker, September 27, 1986.

Danny Dagg attended Smithdeal Massey Business School in Richmond and worked for the U.S. Information Agency, then Rosner Toyota of Fredericksburg after retirement. He died January 18, 2016

Danny Dagg, September 27, 1986.

49

Malone Schooler worked with local developer Carl D. Silver for three years, then in 1977, started his own commercial real estate company, The Malone Schooler CO. He was involved with many fraternal and civic organizations and a generous benefactor to the local community. Music was always a major part of his life – "my

Malone Schooler, September 27, 1986. pre-teen years

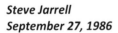

introduced me to Rock and Roll and it never left me." He died on May 9, 2019.

Steve Jarrell
September 27, 1986

Leon Frazier lives in Williamsburg, Virginia. He managed hotels in Richmond for thirteen years, worked with RCA for thirteen years, then was head of government sales for Nextel phones. He still enjoys music and has joined a band in his gated community.

In 2012, he and Steve began performing together whenever Steve has a gig or benefit in Virginia. "We were at the *Dragnet Reunion* at the Armory. I

Leon Frazier, September 27, 1986.

had come home from work, had a glass of wine, called Steve, asked when the show started. He said in two hours, asked me to come. I drove to Fredericksburg and got there fifteen minutes before the show started. Played a whole set."

Last photo of The Prophets together in 2000.
Standing in the same pose as the Fightin' For Sam album cover.
Malone Schooler, Danny Dagg, Ronny Baker, Steve Jarrell and Leon
Frazier. Steve does not remember when the picture was taken, only
that it was at Fairview Beach on their way to Pope's Creek for crabs.

Baby
By Leon Frazier

Oh well my Baby, I here you're putting me down
Oh well come on my baby, you know its' all over town
If you don't love me, like you used to do
Oh well my baby please tell me
So, I can find someone new

Well my baby you left me
And now I'm crying
Over you because you hurt me
But my baby, I still love you

Oh Well my baby, you know I'm hurting inside
Well come on my baby, you don't know how I've tried
And now I'm crying, I'm crying over you
Because my baby, you left me
And you left me so blue

You know you left me blue
Yes you left me so blue
But I still love you

I Still Love You
By Leon Frazier

Well I, I still love you
And I, I- I -I, I still care for you
Oh well you broke my heart and left me sad and blue
Now all I do is cry for you
I cry, I cry…………
Well you, didn't love me anyway
And I, I-I-I think of you night and day
Well you broke my heart and left me sad and blue
Now all I do is cry for you
I cry, I cry…………
Guitar Lead
And now, I'm trying to forget
That girl, that I once met
Oh well she broke my heart and left me sad and blue
Now all I do is cry for you
I cry, I cry
Because I, I still love you
And I-I-I, I still care for you
And I
I still love you
I still love you
I still love you

Fightin' for Sam
By Leon Frazier

I'm sitting here, thinking of a yesterday
When I was oh so free, and I didn't care
I didn't care... air... air I didn't care
Now I'm Locked up here And I can't go anywhere,
Without permission from where
I'm Fightin' for Sam   I'm Fightin' for Sam ...am...am
I'm fightin' for Sam
Well if I could go back just to see my wife
And talk to my son for just one night
But I can't go back cause I've got to stay and fight......
Two Measures
I got a letter, just the other day
It was from my wife, on my son's birthday
On my son's birthday...ah...ah, my son's birthday
It said he's three years old, and he's never seen me
Because here I am, across the Sea
Across the Sea, ...eeee.......eeee   Across the Sea
Well if I could go back just to see my wife
And talk to my son for just one night
But I can't go back cause I've got to stay and fight
Yes, I'm fightin' for Sam, I've got to free this land
I've got to give him a hand
Because I'm fighin'   I'm fightin'   I'm Fightin'
I'm Fightin' for Sam...am....am, Yes I'm fightin' for Sam
Yes, I'm Fightin' for Sam, I've got to free this land
I've got to give him a hand, cause I'm Fightin' for Sam...am.

55

All of My Life
By Leon Frazier

All of my life   All of my life
When you look at me, I get a feeling inside
It's a feeling my dear, that I can't hide
If you knew how I feel, Just thinking our love is real
Then you know, that's all of my life
All of my life....All of my life

When you look at me   With your big brown eyes
I see a love as big, as big as the sky
Then I know that I want you   To Be right by my side
All of my life   That's all of my life

Organ Lead

Then I know that I want you   To be right by my side
All of my life, That's all of my life
When you're not with me   I'm only half a man
And when you not around   I don't know where I stand
That's why I 've got to have you love
Forever and a day
All of my life
That's all of my life   That's all of my life
That's all of my life   That's all of my life
That's all of my life

Feelings Are Just Memories
By Leon Frazier

I can't understand, I just don't know why
You don't seem to care anymore, but you always did before
Know I'm starting to shake, feeling so sick inside
Should I be angry, or go away and cry
And it's too late to say the things that would have meant so
much yesterday
And it's too late to apologize
For all the times I made you cry
Yes I've got to face reality,
All my feelings are just memories
Memories, Memories, Memories

Guitar Lead

Memories of all the times I made you feel so insecure
Memories of all the times I walked right out the door
Memories of all the high-class company that I always keep
But most of all the memories, of all the times I made you
weep
So I call you every day, and I always have nothing to say
I can't believe the coldness in your voice
By now I have no choice
And its' too late to say the things that would have meant so
much yesterday
And its' too late to apologize, for all the times I made you cry
Yes I've go to face reality
All my feelings are just memories

Looking At You from a Distance
By Leon Frazier

I've been looking at you from a distance… I'll never be
noticed from this far
But from here I can see… Much more clearly than you
But I'll never tell you what to do
I felt the hurt you felt when you left your first love
I knew the uneasiness that grew when you lived without love
I was there and I watched as you opened your doors
I was there when you said you had found what you were
looking for
Now is the time to decide, what is best for you
Do you want love just for now, or forever
You've got to make up your mind, there will always be
another time

Sax Lead

I saw the love in your eyes, each time you mentioned his
name
The childless feelings you felt when you played all those
games
Now is the time to decide what is best for you
Do you want love just for now, or forever
You've got to make up your mind
There will always be another time
When I'll be looking at you from a distance
I'll never be noticed from this far
But from here I can see, Much more clearly than you
But I'll never tell you what to do
You know its all up to you….You've got to make up your mind
Girl you have all the time.

All Of My Life was The Prophets' fourth record which they produced as The Prophets Ltd.

The Rotations

"In 1967, free from contractual obligations, the Prophets, under the name The Prophets Ltd. made another recording for a local record label, Look Records. The titles were "All Of My Life," written by Leon Frazier and "I'll Keep Drifting and Dreaming" written by Warren Harding, Jr. owner of Look Records.

"We were like brothers," I quoted Leon's comments to Steve. "We were together all the time. At fraternity parties, practiced together once a week, went to school. Never found the time to get into trouble.

"And we never did drugs. We drank, but no drugs. We tore up a few hotel rooms in New York. One time the guy had to move us three times.

"We also stayed at the same hotel where the Beatles were staying in New York," Leon added. "We never saw them though."

"Leon and Malone had cars," Steve stated, "but it was Pop Baker that drove us to places the most. Around town, to the gigs at Fairview Beach. He had a pickup truck with a camper on the back. One of us would sit in the front with him and the rest would be in back."

But in 1967, The Prophets disbanded.

"Malone was the first to leave. He went into the National Guard that summer. We hired another bass player, but it just wasn't the same."

Unwilling to abandon the group he had started Ronny Baker, with Danny Dagg, continued to keep the band playing for several more years with replacement band members. They were often referred to as Prophets II.

"Leon and I wanted to add horns to the group, but Ronny and Danny didn't, so we left and joined a group called The Rotations.

"They were an eleven-member horn band from Waynesboro that was also playing the *Starlight Pavilion* at Fairview Beach. We played with them for two years.

"The other members were Bob Speck, David Limerick, Billy Gwin, Mike Bliss, Gene Wells, Jim Ring, Mack Marshall, Bobby Driscoll, Bo Martin, Neil Conway, Arthur Myers and John Hutton.

"Back then PA systems were primitive and would have horn speakers like on the football fields. They had no bass quality so you can imagine the sound of seven horn players going through the speakers. The stage at the *Starlight Pavilion* was small like a V-shape and with all eleven of us up there, in a corner at the point, Gene Wells had to sit in the windowsill to play his keyboard.

"If trouble erupted in the club, meaning fights, Mrs. Floyd would make a circle motion with her finger for us to keep playing and not draw attention to what was going on.

"One time, a storm came up, and a boat broke loose from the dock. It was washing downriver toward the pier. Gene saw it coming because he was in the window. He started yelling to Mrs. Floyd and pointing down at the boat. She must have thought there was trouble and signaled to keep playing.

"Next thing we knew, the boat was under the stage and lifted it up, causing us to wobble.

"We would play there on weekends and after the gig, Leon and I returned to our homes in Fredericksburg. Because the rest of the guys lived in Waynesboro, the Floyds furnished them a cottage that had only one bedroom for nine guys. Some would sleep in the cottage, some slept in the band van, others slept on porches of people they knew. This is in the summer and they all shared one bathroom.

"Sometimes the out of town guys hopped in their cars and drove to Maryland to play the slot machines. They would lose all their money in the machines and come back to Virginia.

"Because they didn't have any money, Mrs. Floyd made they clean the beach, pick up trash and rake the sand for hamburgers and hot dogs to survive.

"The following week they'd do the same thing all over again. Everyone was young and didn't care. Leon and I missed all that.

"Like the Prophets, The Rotations also played at fraternity houses.

"UVA was the number one-party school, according to Playboy magazine. We did one party where this guy had a big tub full of grain alcohol and grape juice, you know, purple passion? That was the popular blend of that time.

"It was muddy and raining and the girls were running around in their bras. It was crazy. I remember the band was playing Archie Bell and the Drells' hit 'Tighten Up.' When we got to the words, 'make it mellow' we all dropped our pants. Suddenly there were cameras flashing and somebody put a picture of us in *Life* or *Look* Magazine standing in our underwear!

"In the winter of 1967, UVA had a series of winter concerts and Jackie Wilson and Neil Diamond were doing one of the shows. Remember how I had met Jackie Wilson in New York? When we were the Prophets? Well, I was able to go backstage and talk with Jackie Wilson before the show.

"So, I talked to him for a few minutes and when it was time for him to perform, I got ready to leave. His manager says, 'you can stay because he likes you.'

"I looked over and saw Neil Diamond sitting in the corner, so I went over and started talking to him. This was before Neil became popular."

Steve paused as if reliving the moment.

"There were two things I remember about Neil Diamond. The on and off lights on his amplifier were blue instead of red, and I'd never seen them that way. And his drummer also played with Linda Ronstadt and the Stone Poneys, so the face of his drums had her name on it, not Neil's.

"It had started snowing that night, and the ramp at the back of auditorium was slick. Neil had hired a limo to take those going to the Howard Johnson. The driver was having a hard time getting the limo up the ramp. The wheels kept spinning. Neil said, 'I'll get you out of here.'

"He got behind the wheel, put the car in reverse and crashed into the roll up door, broke the taillights!

"That Monday, I go back to school and I'm telling everybody how I met Neil Diamond, and what he did, and nobody believed me.

"Then, months later, we went on our senior class trip to *The Bitter End*, the oldest nightclub in New York. It's in the middle of Greenwich Village and we went to a show where Tom Posten and Neil Diamond were playing. Neil looked out at the crowd, pointed to me, and said 'I know you'.

"After that I would always take someone with me whenever I thought I might meet somebody important.

"That summer, after graduation, The Rotations took a house gig at *Peabody's Warehouse* in Virginia Beach performing six nights a week. Occasionally, the club would have guests come in. One we backed up was Billy Stewart. His hit 'Summertime' was popular at the time.

"On another occasion, we had The Kingsmen."

Steve started singing some lyrics from "Louie, Louie."

"After the gig, we invited them to a party at a house we had rented. Ended up, the Virginia Beach Police interrupted the party and we were evicted from the house. We had to move to the *Breakers Hotel*.

"That Fall I started at Smithdeal-Massey Business College in Richmond. I rented an apartment with Bob Speck. One night, Mike Bliss, another member of The Rotations visited, said he wanted to discuss the *future* of our music career.

"We decided to start at the top – in New York City. We loaded the van, drove to the big Apple, and applied for jobs at the world-famous *Latin Quarter*. We were hired, not as musicians but the kitchen help.

"We only lasted an hour because the kitchen help spoke a foreign language we couldn't understand. Plus, we were going broke and ended up spending the night at the *Sloan House YMCA*."

Steve chuckled. "You haven't lived until you've stayed in the Sloan House.

"We wired home for money to get back to Richmond. That's when I found out I'd missed too many days from college and wasn't allowed to continue.

"This ended my college career and made me available for the draft.

Graduation day!

The Rotations
Top left, Gene Wells, Arthur Myers, Steve, Bobby Driscoll, Mac
Marshall, Bo Martin, Leon Frazier. Left side holding the trumpet, Mike
Bliss, Bob Speck, Jim Ring. Seated Billy Gwin.

Reunion of The Rotations at Fairview Beach, circa 1988.

Military Days

People hated the military in the 1960's. This was the time of the Vietnam War and no one believed in it.

"One night, we were playing in *Peabody's Warehouse* and my Dad called to say I had a letter from the government. Since I was no longer in college, I suspected it was my draft notice. I told him, 'don't open that letter! I'll be there soon as I finish playing here.'

"I drove all night to Fredericksburg. The next morning, I went to the Air Force recruitment office next door to the post office and said to the guy, 'you see this letter? Sign me up before this postmark.'

"A few days later after a night of partying, I flew out of Richmond and arrived at Lackland Air Force Base in San Antonio, Texas at three in the morning for basic training.

"I was still underage for drinking but during the flight, once we were up in the air, that didn't matter. They served these little bottles of liquor and after drinking them, I decided to keep the empty bottles.

"Anyway, we're in the barracks with the Sergeant," Steve paused. "Sgt. McDonald," he shook his head. "We had to learn how to make our beds military style, you know, with the covers tucked so tight when you threw a quarter on it, the coin flipped to the other side. After we did that, he had us dump our bags onto the beds. Then, he came around and looked at our stuff."

Kay Brooks

He saw the bottles on Steve's bed and hollered, "Whose are these?"

"Mine," Steve answered nervously, "but you can have them if you want."

"You don't tell me what I can do and what I can't do," the Sergeant screamed in my face.

"From then on, I was on his shit list," Steve sighed.

After basic training, Steve went to Tech School at Chanute Air Force Base in Rantoul, Illinois. While there, he met five guys that played together. Steve joined them with his sax, and they called themselves, 4 Carat Blues Band.

"Since military people were looked down upon, I wore a wig whenever I played off base so they couldn't see my close-cropped haircut and know I was in military. When I played on base, I could be a GI.

"The band played at different service clubs on the base and in Champaign, Illinois. I was the only one in the service and worked my regular hours – eight to four or nine to five, I can't remember – and played in the band at nights."

The military also held talent contests and the different squads would compete against one another. Steve's Squad Commander heard he played the sax and called him into his office.

"I understand you're a sax player," he said. He told Steve about the talent contest, said he wanted Steve to enter.

"What's in it for me?" Steve challenged. "I asked if I could be excused from some of the duties. Said it was hard to get up in the morning after playing all night. The Commander agreed to my terms – provided I won.

"I had just taught myself to play two saxophones at the same time, so that's what I did. And won the contest." Steve gave me a broad smile. "And the Commander wrote me a note.

"The next morning, the Drill Sgt. came in and was ordering everyone around. I stayed in my bed. When he started hollering at me, I just handed him my note."

Steve laughs. "I remember him stomping out of the barracks and slamming the door behind him. From that time on, I was responsible for the luggage room. I still had to go to class, but I didn't have to march."

Steve in his dress uniform when he graduated from basic training.

Steve outside the barracks.

Top Row left to right: The Lt, ? McDonald, Dan Tremere, Larry Hoyer,
Terry Seaward, Warren Marchek, Evan Fluth. Bottom row, left to right:
David Jackson, Doug Diemer, Max Sanchez, Steve, David Buono,
Darrell Bushek.

John Winterhalder and Tom Wightman who served with
Steve at March Air Force Base in Riverside, California.

"After tech school, I was stationed at March Air Force Base in Riverside, California where I was good friends with John Winterhalder and Tom Wightman.

"I also had a tough Sergeant, Sgt. Luby Guillot. He's the one that made a man out of me. You have to remember; I was a cocky nineteen-year-old at the time. Sgt. Guillot taught me a lot about many things, how to be responsible and grow up. You can imagine how I felt when I went to Thailand and he was there as well. Now I can say he was very important in my life.

"Once again, I found a band. They were an all Mexican band called the Highlighters and those guys could speak English as good as me but anytime people would complain about our music being too loud or the selection of songs, they'd pretend they didn't understand and point to me! I had to take all the heat.

"One time we were playing at this big Mexican wedding reception and there was this twelve-year old boy there dressed in a tuxedo. He walked under a water sprinkler and got soaked. We were taking a break and when I saw him, I laughed. It must have hurt his feelings because he went to some of his relatives and said I was picking on him. One of the guys in the band got wind of it and told me I needed to leave. Quick. The relatives were coming to beat me up. That was the last time I saw that band.

"Riverside is where I met Dick Dale, the father of surf music.

"He owned a club near the base and performed there with his wife Jeanne. They had a routine like Sonny and Cher. On Monday nights, Dick Dale had a 'do your thing night' and allowed musicians to sit in and perform with his group so, I decided to participate.

"One week I played my sax. The next week I played and sang. Dick offered me a job in his band The Deltones and once again, I was turning wrenches by day for the Air Force and playing music at night with the band.

"When I got my orders for Thailand, Dick wrote a letter to try and get me excused but it didn't work. My last night, before I left, Dick said, 'when you get out of the service, I want you to come play with me.'"

*MSGT Luby Guillot.
Steve's Sergeant at March Air Force Base in Riverside and U-Tapao Air Base in Thailand.*

Steve and Dan Tremere. Taken at a Sons of the Beach show; the first time they had seen each other since 1968 in tech school at Chanute Air Force Base. Rantoul, IL

Salt & Pepper

In August 1969, Steve was transferred to South East Asia at U-Tapao Air Base in Sattahip, Thailand, ninety miles south of Bangkok.

"That's where I met Tony Nardi. He played keyboard and was putting together a band. He had already recruited Ed Mobley as lead singer, Jim Plummer was on guitar, Dan Sullivan who played bass and BT Bailey who played drums. I auditioned and signed on with my sax and sang.

"We were a soul and rhythm and blues band. Called ourselves Salt & Pepper because of the mixed races, which was rare in those days.

By October, Salt & Pepper was ready to go live.

"We performed off-duty at Officer's Clubs, on military bases, in army camps. We travelled all over Thailand. Then we were hired to play every other Saturday night at *Jack's American Star Bar*, a Thai Soul Food Restaurant in Bangkok.

"One Saturday night I met O. C. Smith. His song, 'Little Green Apples' had just made number two on the Billboard Hits."

Jack's American Star Bar was owned by William Herman "Jack" Jackson a retired Army Sergeant who remained in Bangkok and married a Thai woman. It featured soul music, spicy food, sexy dancers and was popular with the black GI's in Thailand.

"Jack Jackson talked Leslie 'Ike' Atkinson, another retired master sergeant into joining him and I didn't know until years later that they ran a heroin drug ring together. The drugs were concealed in duffle bags and overnight bags.

"Do you remember the movie AMERICAN GANGSTER? It's based on the sting that brought them down.

"Back then, soldiers had these AWOL bags they could use whenever they travelled. At that time, these AWOL bags were never searched at the airports. The bags had secret compartments and that was how the drugs were moved.

"I found this out years later when I was reading an article by Ron Chepesiuk stating he was writing a book about Ike Atkinson and his band of brothers. I looked Chepesiuk up and called him. Told him I had been a member of the Salt & Pepper band and we played at *Jack's American Star Bar*. He ended up interviewing me and mentioned me and the band on pages 90 and 92 in the book, *Sergeant Smack: The Legendary Lives and Times of Ike Atkinson, Kingpin, and his Band of Brothers.*"

Steve pointed to the bookcase. "I've got the book on the shelf over there. I also had Ron Chepesiuk and Ike Atkinson on one of my radio shows."

He shook his head. "All this was going on while we played there, and we never knew about it."

Salt & Pepper also played at *Charlie's Hideaway Restaurant,* an exclusive Thai resort in Pattaya Beach, and Grand Hotel in Bangkok, Thailand.

"We worked during the day, got off-hours gigs and were the first band to open clubs. We lived off base, had bungalows and travelled in cars and vans everywhere.

"Ed Mobley had written some songs and in early 1970, we recorded 'Linda' and 'Man of My Word,' at the Sri Krueng Recording Studio in Bangkok. We were the first Americans to ever record in Southeast Asia, so I've been told.

"We put the songs on Tony Nardi's label, Heatwave Records. Ordered the minimum amount, 500 copies, I think, and sold them or gave them away at gigs. It received air play on Armed Forces Radio and the BBC English Language Radio in Bangkok.

"It was also featured in the *Stars and Stripes* military newspaper."

Forty years later "Man of My Word" became a hit in the *Northern Soul Movement* in Europe and was released on a compilation of recordings on the Kent Record Label.

"You know, I never started smoking until I went to Thailand and lived on a B-52 Bomber base. I will never forget when I first arrived there. I had three roommates and we lived in small cubicle. The other guys had been there a few months and he was initiated really quick. They had already gotten used to the sound of the planes coming in for a landing. One night, a plane was coming in and one of my roommates became nervous because it didn't sound like one of ours. Me, being the new guy, it really got me upset. Scared is the word!"

"Here, Steve," another roommate handed him a cigarette, "have a cigarette. It will calm you down."

"Well, it didn't. I told him to give me another. The next day, I bought a carton. It took me 34 years to get off them. I tried to stop many times. Finally, about ten years ago, I went to Boston and saw Yefim Shubentsov, the Mad Russian. He had cured, Billy Joel, Drew Barrymore, and half the cast of the TV show *Friends*, from smoking. He did some sort of strange thing, waved his hand in my face, blew in my face, but when I walked out of there it was like I had never smoked.

"At the end of our tour – when everybody's year was up – we all went our separate ways and Salt & Pepper disbanded."

Salt & Pepper
"Taken in the Airmen's Club at U-Tapao Airbase in Sattahip,
Thailand. We played there, Bangkok and Pattaya Beach."

·Ed Mobley, Tony Nardi and Steve, the surviving members of Salt
and Pepper, at a reunion in Alamosa, CO in 2015 after hearing that
their 1969 recording of "Man Of My Word' had become a hit in
Europe in the Northern Soul Movement.

This is Steve Jarrell, chief saxophonist and acrobat with the Salt and Pepper band, the rock group that comes up from Sattahip every weekend to play at Jack's American Star Bar on the Strip. Salt and Pepper, generally regarded as the top band in this part of town, was formed six months ago by US servicemen at Sattahip.

From "Bangkok Nights & Daze" article by Louie Morales, in the Bangkok Post, May 6, 1970.

Steve was reassigned to Plattsburgh Air Force Base in Plattsburg, New York where he became friends with fellow servicemen, Bill Cashel and Rusty Scarborough.

"Bill was from Long Island, New York and stays in touch. Rusty was from Durham, North Carolina and kept in touch up to his passing."

Steve also met Art Gebo, leader of the house band in the Cabaret Club on Lake Champlain. They called themselves Cabaret Brass & Co.

"I became their lead singer and sax player and again, I'm doing my Air Force job during the day and performing every night.

"Bill Cashel and Rusty Scarborough would ride to the club with me every night and party while I was performing. From there we would go to the pizzeria then back to the barracks at three in the morning. We would get up at seven to be at work at eight. Lunch hours were spent back at the barracks sleeping for an hour We would catch another couple hours' sleep after work then back to work that night at the club. I remember one morning, standing at attention at roll call and Rusty passed out and fell in the floor.

"Also, Bill was getting out of the service and never took his hat off because he didn't want to have short hair when he got out. He would stuff his long hair inside his cap and never signed off base without his cap on. I still

Bill Cashel, one of Steve's two "running" buddies at Plattsburgh AFB in Plattsburgh, NY.

stay in touch with Bill to this day.

"One evening, I met the Warden of Dannemora State Prison. I asked if they ever allowed live entertainment for the prisoners. The answer was 'no'."

Cabaret Brass & Co. were the first group to perform inside the prison. "We took three 'go-go' girls with us and the inmates loved it!"

A fond memory of Plattsburg was when the Beach Boys came to do a show at NY State University. "A friend told me the Beach Boys were staying at the hotel where she worked. I called the hotel and left a message for Mike Love telling him I was former Sax player for Dick Dale and the Deltones. Mike invited me over to the hotel to visit, asked me if I was going to the show. When I answered it was closed to the public and only for students, Mike said I could go with them. I hopped in the car with them and watched the show from backstage. This was when Daryl Dragon and Toni Tennille sang with in the group. After the show, while they were tearing down the equipment, Dennis Wilson and I tossed a frisbee back and forth across the stage. That's the last time I saw Dennis before he drowned in 1983."

Months later, Steve was relocated back to U-Tapao Airfield in Thailand.

Before leaving, Steve returned to Fredericksburg to visit with family and friends. This visit was mentioned during my interview with John Faulkner.

"Steve and I have been lifelong friends and when he got those orders for the second tour, I was worried I might never see him again. So, I decided we would spend some quality time together and offered to drive Steve to Riverside, California. Encouraged Tommy Mitchell to join us.

"At the time, they didn't sell Coors beer east of the Mississippi so when we crossed over the river, we stopped and bought enough beer to last us for months. That was our biggest accomplishment – driving all night and drinking Coors beer.

"We travelled over two thousand miles in three days in my '64 Volkswagen. We couldn't afford to stay in motels but camped and slept in our sleeping bags. The first night, it was late, and dark, when we stopped. The next morning, we were awakened by the rumble and loud noise of a train. We had no idea we were camped near some railroad tracks!

"The second night, we stopped in Missouri. We noticed the 'bears' sign but didn't really pay any attention to it. The next morning Tommy Mitchell was awakened to what he thought was a black bear licking his face. It turned out to be a big black dog! Tommy was screaming and Steve and I were rolling out our sleeping bags laughing."

"That was one adventurous trip," Steve agreed, "and I just appreciate my two friends spending the time with me.

"When I got to Thailand, Salt & Pepper was no longer together but I hooked up with a band called The Internationals, made up of guys from all over the world. I played a couple gigs with them in Bangkok."

One night, after a late show, the band slept in one of the rooms behind the stage. "It was like a dorm room with several bunk beds in it. I awoke in the middle of night, overheard two of the guys in the band talking. One of them had a grocery sack half full of test tube vials."

Steve paused to be sure I realized he was talking about drugs.

"*Let me get out of here*, I thought to myself. I grabbed my stuff and left right then. This was in 1971 and I did not want to spend the rest of my life in a Thai prison."

Months later, Steve's tour was cut short when he learned his stepfather had terminal cancer. "I was released from the Air Force to return to be with my mother during this sad time.

"Shortly after I arrived in Winston Salem, NC, I met these guys that had a little band called Potpourri. I performed with them until my stepfather passed."

Steve also crossed paths with singer Ronnie Dove.

"I knew Ronnie from The Prophets days and would sometimes sit in with his band in Waldorf, Maryland.

"Ronnie wanted me and my drummer friend Mike Shiflett from Richmond to come to Nashville and work with his agent Bill Sizemore.

"Bill assigned Mike and me to go on the road and perform with Ruby and The Romantics for a tour of the states and Sondrestrom, Greenland.

"Mike and I hooked up with The Romantics in Cincinnati, Ohio at the Viking Lounge to rehearse before leaving for Greenland. The club was an African American night club and The Romantics were all white. We had to perform a set before Ruby came on stage.

"We walked in to play and somebody from the audience said, 'what are you doing in here white boy?' Another said, 'what are you going to play whitey?'

"I sang every soul song I knew. We were supposed to play for a week, but they ended up holding us over an extra week.

"Then we went to Sondrestrom for six weeks. That was the coldest place I have ever been.

"We met some Air Force guys that flew small planes and they took us to the Polar Ice Cap, the top of the world. We flew between mountains of ice. There were so many beautiful colors. Blue. Green. Turquois and white.

"When we returned to the U.S., Ruby and The Romantics were booked in Birmingham, Alabama in a hotel lounge.

"Ruby was African-American, and the club manager was white. The hotel owners found out Ruby and the club manager were married. I got a call in my hotel room from the front desk telling me I had fifteen minutes to get out. The owners had fired everybody associated with the club.

"Mike Shiflett returned to Virginia and Bill Sizemore sent me to work with a band called Pride & Joy in Chicago, Illinois.

"Pride & Joy was the backup band for Joy Brittan, a headliner night club performer from Canada. She was booked for three weeks at the Fields Supper Club in Chicago.

"The band members were Mike Papa from New York City, John Unger and Richie Van from Windsor, Ontario, Canada and me. We played the first week and had a day off. Joy had a disagreement with the management and when we returned to play the following Monday night, Joy, the star of the show, had left town! We persuaded the manager to allow us to stay and perform without her. Mike Papa and I had been front men in bands. We threw a show together that afternoon and played to the end of the three-week contract.

"When I returned to Winston Salem, after that gig, I remember standing in line at a fast food restaurant."

"Steve Jarrell," this voice behind me hollered.

"I looked around but didn't recognize anyone. Then a fellow tapped me on the shoulder.

"You don't know me, do you?"

"There was this long haired, bearded, hippy-looking guy in bib overalls."

"I'm Larry Miller," he said.

"If you remember, Larry was the piano player I performed with when I was in the fourth grade at Beulah Elementary School. He was playing with a band called Revelation from Greensboro, NC.

"Revelation was owned by Jim Lowry and his wife Sylvia. Their sax player, Craig Woolard, had just left the group to join The Embers, so Larry introduced me to Jim and Sylvia. They hired me to join the band and I played with them for a short period before leaving to go back to California, where I joined Dick Dale.

Cabaret and Company.
The first group to perform inside a state prison.

Steve singing with Pride & Joy.

Dick Dale and the Deltones

Dick Dale – Richard Anthony Monsour – was the undisputed father of surf music before the Beach Boys, Jan and Dean, any of those acts.

He started out in country music but after playing with the guitar sounds and constantly blowing up his *Fender* amplifiers, he collaborated with the company to produce custom-made 100-watt guitar amplifiers.

Being left-handed, he outfitted his gold Stratocaster guitar to suit his style. It played loudly and was named "the Beast."

The Beatles invasion and health issues created a sporadic music career but several of his songs were featured in Annette Funicello and Frankie Avalon's BEACH PARTY and MUSCLE BEACH PARTY movies. He and the band performed the songs in the movies. His "Misirlou" is the first song you hear in the movie PULP FICTION.

"Dick Dale was inducted into the Musicians Hall of Fame and Museum in Nashville and the Surfing Walk of Fame in Huntington Beach, California," Steve said. "He played until his death in March 2019 at the age of 81.

"While living in Winston Salem and playing with the Revelations, I kept thinking of his offer to play with him and the Deltones so I gave him a call to say 'hello.'

"Dick repeated his offer. Since Revelation was a part-time, weekend band and I needed a full-time job, I decided to join the group.

"Dick had sold the Club in Riverside, California and was touring the country. He and Jeanne, his wife, had a big house on the Balboa Peninsula in Newport Beach and no children. Since I needed a place to live, they invited me to stay there with them.

"I have to say, those were wonderful times.

I learned more about the music business from Dick Dale than anybody in music.

"We would go to the beach almost every day, have lunch often at a place called *The Little Pickle* in Huntington Beach and play music!

"Dick studied karate with the legendary instructor Ed Parker. So did Elvis Presley, and Elvis and Dick became good friends.

"I never met Elvis. He never came to the house, but Dick would go visit him.

"Dick's wife, Jeanne, studied karate with Mike Stone, another instructor. Priscilla Presley studied with Mike too and the two women became friends.

"This was when Elvis and Priscilla split up and Priscilla would come to the house and visit Jeanne. She would bring Lisa Marie with her. I guess she was about three or four. While Priscilla and Jeanne sat around the kitchen table talking, I would be on the floor playing with Lisa Marie and her toys or putting her on my shoulders, riding her around the room.

"Dick liked exotic pets. He had a four-hundred-pound African lion and many nights we would be eating dinner and that lion would be chomping chicken legs on the floor beside us."

John Faulkner mentioned visiting Dick Dale before Steve went to Thailand the second time.

"Dick Dale drove a big Rolls Royce and anytime he went to the shopping centers, he would park it on the sidewalk outside the store. He would go in the store and we would watch people stopping to look at the car outside. I guess they thought it was on display."

Steve, Dick Dale and the Deltones played Las Vegas, up and down the California coast and as far east as Kansas City.

"Whenever we were in the Los Angeles area, the karate guys would come to the show, then to the house afterwards. They would start showing each other karate moves and use me as their dummy since I knew nothing about karate. They would say, 'don't move and you won't get hurt.'

"I'd stand there, and they'd kick all around me. One of the guys was Chuck Norris. He was just an instructor then. This was before he was in the movies.

"Another highlight was when we were on our way to a club owner's birthday party, Dick received a phone call from a friend that was having car trouble and needed a ride. It turned out to be Bill Medley of The Righteous Brothers. I was a big Righteous Brothers fan, so I was thrilled.

"Then we went to Hawaii to play for six weeks at a popular night spot on Kalakaua Avenue in Waikiki called *The Beef 'n' Grog*. It had tables inside and outside along the sidewalk and open-air windows. A friend Paul Bruening, we sometimes called him 'PB,' who I had not seen in years was living in Hawaii and was a pharmacist.

"Remember the Rotations? After the Prophets? Gene Wells was the keyboard player in the Rotations and PB was Gene's roommate in college. PB often travelled with us during The Rotation days.

"Anyway, PB happened to be riding his scooter down Kalakaua Avenue and heard the music coming out of the *Beef and Grog* club. He pulled to the curb to listen. I was singing 'Precious and Few' and PB said, 'that sounds like Steve Jarrell!'

"He came inside and sure enough, there I was. PB was living in Kahala, the other side of Diamond Head in a six-bedroom house with four other guys.

"One of the roommates had moved back to the mainland and PB asked if I would be interested in the empty bedroom. He said the rent would be $300 a month for my share.

"I jumped at the opportunity, left the Deltones and moved in with them.

"Hawaii had a strict union rule and musicians could only play casual for a year before they could play full time. I played part time with a jam band in a club. We called ourselves 'The Unknown Band.'

"For income, I worked at the Palm Beach clothing store in the Ala Moana Shopping Center in Honolulu. One day, a guy came in and said he was looking for some extras for the original TV series Hawaii Five O.

"In one episode, 'Danno' was chasing a bad guy in a tall parking garage and the bad guy jumped over the railing. They had a mattress on top of empty boxes down below where he was supposed to land. We were all making bets where he would end up. He does the scene, the camera picks up with a crowd rushing around the body, and I'm in the crowd."

Steve laughed. "Small part. I didn't get paid for it but got invited to the wrap party at Jack Lord's condo after a week of filming. The main thing I remember was Joey Heatherton was there.

"Then I woke up one morning thinking about the fall and football weather in Virginia. I thought about it all day and guess I got homesick. One of my roommates worked for an airline and I asked him if he could get me a hardship ticket so I could fly home. He did and I flew back to Virginia.

"Never to return to Hawaii again."

Dick Dale and the Del-Tones.
Left to right: Steve, Billy McBride, Jeanne Dale, Dick Dale, John Gentusa, Robbie Thompson.

Dick Dale and Elsa the Lion.   *Autographed picture, 1994.*

Dick Dale's home on Balboa Peninsula in Newport Beach, California.

Steve and Paul "PB" Bruening in Hawaii.

The Diplomats and Surprise

Steve left Hawaii returned to Fredericksburg and looked up some of his musician friends.

"I needed a job and started playing with The Diplomats, one of the most talented groups I've ever played with. They were more than a group of local guys. Steve Brown, the leader was a great singer. Emory Shover played his guitar with more enthusiasm than I have ever seen anybody play an instrument. Richard Mason never made a mistake on bass. There was also Danny Jones and Mike Burnett. Darwin Golding was a good singer and drummer. And it was also fun to play with Jimmy Adams, the guy that taught me how to play the sax.

They were a fun group and played every weekend at the *Starlight Pavilion* in Fairview Beach and I felt like I had come full circle."

Months later, a new Holiday Inn was built on Route 17 just North of Fredericksburg. Steve learned they were going to have a lounge – *Escadrille Lounge* – for entertainment.

"By this time, I was playing music full time. I had the opportunity to put a house band together with Pat Moore, David Limerick, Darwin Golding and myself. We called ourselves Surprise and played six nights a week for six months. We had a faithful following, one of them being Nick Nichols from our Prophets days. Nick was now married and he and his wife, Emma, enjoyed doing synchronized dancing every week.

"Then I was offered an opportunity to play a house gig at the *Fisherman's Restaurant and Lounge* in Virginia Beach. David Limerick went with me. We hooked up with two other musicians, Jim Spivey who played guitar and Gary Kirkland on drums.

"It was just for the summer months and we played soul and R&B. I remember one night this lady hollered, 'sing it again, Steve, sing it again.'

Karma to Surprise.
Karma was the first name of the band, then it was changed to Surprise. Left to right, David Limerick, Steve, Darwin Golden and Pat Moore. Surprise was the first band to open in the Escadrille Lounge in the Holiday Inn North in Fredericksburg, Virginia. They played there six nights a week for six months.

Our House

"That Fall I got the opportunity to be a vocalist and sax player for one of the top show bands in the Southeast, Our House. They worked 48 weeks out of the year from Cape Cod, Massachusetts to Miami Florida.

"They worked with the Fred Petty Agency out of Boston. Some of the members – Bob Speck, Billy Gwin and Mike Bliss – had been with The Rotations. John and Danny Hines, Greg Geis and Bruce Gavlik were added to the group. When they started going through personnel changes, I was asked to join them.

"While playing in Myrtle Beach, South Carolina we met a man named Stan Hardin. Stan was a chiropractor, but he also played the guitar and wrote songs.

"He had written a song, 'Mr. Magic Man' and wanted us to record it. We agreed and travelled to Charlotte, North Carolina and recorded in the Reflections Studio.

"We needed a *B*-side to the 45 RPM record and decided to record the Drifters' hit 'Up On The Roof.'

"Since we were all fans of Bill Deal and the Rhondels, we decided to record it in their style. The record wasn't released until ten years later, and by then, Our House had disbanded.

"By the end of 1974, we were playing New Year's Eve at *Pete and Lenny's* in Ft. Lauderdale, Florida. It was an all disco club and I realized the well-known show group Our House was having to become a disco band and more and more of the clubs we played were discos.

"My New Year's Resolution that year was that I would never play disco again. Then, out of the blue, my high school buddy, Jimmy Franklin, offered me part ownership in a hotel management corporation in Fredericksburg.

"The timing couldn't have been better. I took the offer, left Our House, and returned to Virginia.

Our House
Top: Billy Gwin. Standing, left to right: Danny Hines, Steve,
Bob Speck, John Hines. On floor: Mike Bliss

The General Washington Inn

The General Washington Inn is built over the foundation of the colonial home of Mildred Washington, aunt and godmother to George Washington, our first U.S. President. It was originally called The Stratford Hotel and owned by James G. Gore, uncle to Vice-President Al Gore until 1962 when Harry Franklin and his realtor partners bought it.

Famous people have stayed there – Frank Sinatra, Dean Martin, Joey Bishop to name a few. Marine officers and UVA coeds have danced many Wednesday, Friday, and Saturday nights in the Jockey Club there.

Harry Franklin offered his son Jimmy the hotel to manage because it would be easier to sell an operating business than an empty deteriorating building.

"Jimmy called me; offered me the option to run the two nightclubs on the facility. David Limerick was also burned out from performing, so Jimmy offered David a position as well. Jimmy would manage the hotel, David the restaurant, and I would oversee the two bars."

Returning to the General Washington Inn brought back memories of Steve's youth. "I remembered working there a couple summers and hanging out at the pool after work."

High school classmate, Nicky Seay's mother managed the Inn for many years. Nicky shared some of those memories with me.

"I lived there in high school," Nicky stated in my phone interview, "until I left for graduate school in 1972. I worked there as a lifeguard in the summers and would let a lot of the guys and girls inside to swim in the afternoons and evenings.

"One summer I managed to get jobs for nine of my friends. They were front desk clerks, night auditors, bus boys, servers, you name it. They would work during the day, then hang out by the pool in the evenings."

Nicky chuckled. "I remember the restaurant cook fussing at the guys. 'Just because you work here doesn't mean you can eat all of my guests' cinnamon buns and biscuits by the dozens!'"

I asked Nicky what it was like to be friends with Steve.

"He was like a rock star. Going places and doing things. But he never got above his friends. To this day, he has always favored his friends and whenever he is in Fredericksburg, he values the time he spends with us. We also talk fairly often."

Back to Steve.

"Jimmy, David and I had big plans for the Inn. It already had a small bar downstairs called the *Jockey Club* that had been exclusive for years, so we didn't change that. On the Main floor was a large room that was previously used by a private members-only social organization. We changed it into a club and called it the *Cherry Tree.*

"We had a lighted dance floor, slides showing on the walls, a DJ booth, and a large stage. Offered live entertainment with some big-name bands – The Coasters, Archie Bell and the Drells, Herman's Hermits, The Association, Bill Deal and the Rhondels, Brooklyn Bridge just to name a few.

"Unfortunately, the *Cherry Tree* was too successful. Better than the restaurant, in fact. You see, alcohol could not comprise more than fifty-five percent of the food sales. We sold more than the Department of Alcohol Beverage Control allowed and they pulled our license.

"It was downhill from there and we were quickly going broke!"

This was also around the time Steve decorated one of Barry Sullivan's townhouse bedrooms.

"Steve had had some of the Washington Redskins linebackers at the General Washington Inn talking about football," Barry explained. "Steve and a couple of the guys decided to go out afterwards. I went home because I had to work the next day.

"At two AM they showed up at my townhouse at Olde Greenwich with these green glowsticks. You know, those party sticks you shake, and they glow in the dark. Well, they had punched holes in them and charged into my bedroom swinging them all over the place.

"What are you doing, I shouted.

"Steve laughed, 'don't worry, it will dry up and disappear.'

"The next morning, I woke up and had these green dots all over my bedroom. The walls, ceiling, the furniture, my closet, my clothes. Even my hair!"

Picture Postcard of The General Washington Inn in Fredericksburg, Virginia.

Stevie Wonder

"I met Stevie Wonder in 1973. I remember because 'Superstition' was released in 1972 and this was shortly after that.

"I was living in Richmond at the time and on a break from Our House.

"My cousin Tommy Jarrell was General Manager at my uncle's Truck Plaza and always looking for ways to promote the Plaza. He and a couple other businesses were sponsoring a series of concerts and had hired Stevie to do three shows – one in Richmond, one in Norfolk and one somewhere else. Chuck Berry was also supposed to be there, but he never showed up.

"That afternoon I went with Tommy to the Convention Center in Richmond when they were setting up. I had just bought a big bass sax and told Harold Williams about it. Harold was a sax player for the Goose Creek Symphony that was also on the show. He had never seen one so I said I would bring it with me that evening.

"I was backstage after the show, playing it for everybody and Stevie Wonder heard me from his dressing room next door. He wanted to know what the instrument was and sent one of his guys to invite me to come play for him.

"Stevie says, 'I'm going to be in Norfolk tomorrow night, why don't you come on down.

"Remember how I said I was going to take someone with me whenever I met anybody important? Well, I took Jimmy

Franklin with me. He was bartending at the *Escadrille Lounge* when I was there.

"Stevie was staying at *The Scope* and after the Norfolk concert, he invited Jimmy Franklin and me to his room. I had the horn with me, and Stevie had an electric piano in the room. We drank Mateus wine and sang Otis Redding songs until five in the morning.

"It was a great time but the thing I remember most was Stevie had all his albums in Braille.

"Stevie and I became good friends. At the time, he was living at the Plaza Hotel in New York. We called each other often and I visited him whenever I was in New York.

Once, Stevie asked, "what are you going to do now?"

"I guess I'll go back on the road," I responded.

Stevie said, "if you ever need anything, just give me a call."

On August 6, 1973, Stevie Wonder was in a horrific auto accident on his way to a benefit performance in Durham, N.C. The car ran into the back of a flatbed log truck and Stevie was in a coma for four days. He moved to the West Coast after that and Steve lost track of him.

Years later, when Steve lived in Nashville, his father came to visit.

"I was playing with Donna Fargo at the time and back then, if you sang with one of the stars, you could go backstage at the *Grand Ole Opry*.

"So, I took my dad. We were leaving and Stevie and his entourage were coming in. I think he was in town for a black music conference. I spoke to Stevie and he recognized my voice. I introduced him to my Dad. Told Dad about Stevie's offer that if I ever needed anything, to give him a call."

"I haven't heard from you," Stevie responded.

"I haven't done anything important enough to bother you with."

"Well, the offer still stands," Stevie remarked.

"I thought a minute, then said, 'there is one thing you can do for me. Take a picture with me and my Dad.'

"And that's what he did."

Stevie Wonder, Steve and his Dad, Arlon Jarrell at the Grand Ole Opry.

Spiral Starecase

Steve left the General Washington Inn in 1977 when he got the call to audition for Spiral Starecase. They were originally a five-member band from Sacramento, California called the Fydallions and formed in 1964 for an Air Force talent contest.

The band members were Dick Lopes on sax, Bobby Raymond, bass guitar, Harvey Kaye keyboards, Vinnie Parello, drums, and Pat Upton, guitar and lead vocals.

"They went on the road after getting out of the service and had a monster hit – 'More Today than Yesterday.'

"I think the hits were with Columbia Records who made them change their name. They chose the title of the movie, *Spiral Staircase* but got creative and altered the spelling to *starecase*.

"They were popular in 1969 and would have been more successful if they hadn't had a crooked manager who mismanaged their funds. They only lasted about eighteen months. Pat Upton left and joined Ricky Nelson.

"Anyway, by 1977, Harvey Kaye, the band leader decided he wanted to revive the band and his partner at the time, Fred Weis called me. Asked if I would be interested in auditioning for the lead singer. Fred lived in Florida, so I went down there, auditioned, and got the job.

"We rehearsed in Miami then went on the road. There were two girls – Debby Ryan and Demarus Whitewing. They sang background and it was my job to look out for the girls as well as sing.

"In August 1977, I will never forget it because it was right after Elvis died, we played in a hotel where The Commodores and The Emotions were staying. After their concert, they came to the club where we were playing and jammed with us until two in the morning.

"Then Harvey Kaye decided to leave the group and put a band together in Las Vegas where he lived.

"Bands are always changing members but in order to keep their names, at least one member has to be an original member. When Harvey Kaye left, there were no originals in the Spiral Starecase band, and I was feeling a little uneasy.

"Another downside was after one of our gigs, we witnessed a patron get in a scuffle with the club manager and fall out an eighth-floor window, killing him. We were all taken to the police station where the police spent the entire night taking our statements. That was the straw that broke the camel's back for me. I decided I needed to quit the road for a while.

"I was tired, and things were getting too crazy. I decided to come back to Virginia, change careers and play music as a hobby.

"An interesting side story...years later when I was producing oldies shows, Pat Upton, the original lead singer did some of the shows with us. Pat knew that I had been one of the singers in the group after he left and we used to joke about it because I would say 'Hey Pat, I used to be you!'

"Pat was a great guy. He lived in Alabama and was always there for the benefit shows we did for the ailing music stars."

Spiral Starecase
Steve cannot remember the names of the guys. He is in the center. Girls:
Debbie Ryan on left, Demaris Whitewing on right.

Fire #1

Steve's uncle, Oran Jarrell, owned *Jarrell's Truck Plaza,* a large industrial complex North of Richmond in Doswell, Virginia. Steve's cousin Tommy Jarrell was the General Manager.

"I went to Tommy and said I was ready for a normal job — if there is such a thing.

"I started pumping gas, then worked in the store; became store manager, then motel manager. My uncle decided he wanted to open a fast food restaurant on the property and bought a *Burger Chef* franchise.

"He sent me to 'Hamburger College' in Cincinnati, Ohio for three weeks. I returned and became the restaurant manager.

"That first year, I had the #1 *Burger Chef* in the nation because of the sign on the interstate and the closest restaurant was in Ashland. Plus, we were across from the entrance to *King's Dominion* a popular amusement park. Location was the key."

Steve chuckled. "This was about the time Billy Kain gave me another name. In addition to Rootie, he called me the 'burger baron of Doswell.'"

"Speaking of *King's Dominion,* they had a roller coaster there called the *Rebel Yell.* Actor George Segal was making the movie ROLLER COASTER and did a promotion for the movie at Kings Dominion. *Guinness Book of World Records* was also hosting a contest to see who could stay on the roller coaster the longest. I entered the contest and rode through the first lap with George Segal. Then he got off and I stayed on. It amazed me that George Segal's hair was sprayed so much that it didn't move during the whole roller coaster ride!

"Also, there was a national roller coaster riding club that travelled all over the country entering the contests. These guys were so serious they had one-two men pit crews.

"I wore a football helmet to keep my head from rocking around and managed to stay on for 14 hours which turned out to be 348 miles.

"Another highlight was the truck plaza owned a limousine and whenever a VIP came to town, I would drive the limo to pick them up at the Richmond Airport. One of the guys was Barry Goldwater.

"On another occasion, I picked up Andy Gibb and drove him to his first American concert at Kings Dominion. I stood on the stage as he sang. Watched the girls throw candy, gifts and underwear onstage. I remember he nervously look over at me as I smiled and laughed.

"Despite changing careers, I couldn't stay away from music. I started playing with the Johnny Wayne Trio at the *Virginia Inn* in Richmond every weekend.

"Johnny Wayne Robinson was well known in the Richmond area and we packed the Club every week. Unlike most hotel lounges, this one was like a Country Club. The same people frequented it every weekend and everybody knew everybody.

"On the evening of September 3, 1978, I left my home in Richmond to go to the Fredericksburg Fair with some friends. I spent the night in Fredericksburg and drove back to Richmond only to find that my house had burned down.

"My brother, Stan, and PB were living with me at the time and I'll never forget pulling up to the house and seeing Stan, PB, Billy Kain and Robert Chinn sitting on the step waiting for me.

"Whoever owned the house before me had converted the attached garage into a recreation room. Because it didn't have heating or air conditioning, I was using a window air conditioner and the wiring shorted out, caught the couch on fire. There were several other houses that burned the same way. Billy Kain was working with the Virginia State Police by then and I remember they were Investigating to determine if there were any contractor connections.

"Leon Frazier was managing the Howard Johnson at the time and arranged for me to stay at the hotel until I could find a new home.

"The hotel had a 24-hour coffee shop and I was sitting there late one night when Bob Seger and his band came in. They had just done a concert in Richmond and were staying at the hotel.

"I started a conversation with them and explained that my home had burned and all I had left was a suitcase of clothes and two saxophones in the trunk of my car. Someone said, 'I think the Man upstairs,' as he pointed up, 'is trying to tell you something.'

"I had already made an offer to buy a new home through a Veterans Administration loan, only to find out because I was attempting to move into a gated community, the VA wouldn't approve it. They inferred that a gated community was segregated.

"In the failed effort to buy another home, I started to think there might be some merit to what Bob Segar's bandmember told me. I called Dick Dale, explained what had happened and he said to come back to California, play with his band again.

"So, I gave my notice to the family at the Truck Plaza and the day after Thanksgiving, left again for California.

"My friends Jim and Sylvia Lowry from the Revelation Band had moved to Nashville, Tennessee by then, and I stopped to visit with them on the way.

"Jim had been hired to play guitar in Donna Fargo's band and when I stopped by to see them, Jim told me Donna was looking to hire a new background singer. He asked if I would audition.

"I was hired and became a member of the Donna Fargo Band.

"There was a problem, though. Donna was working on the West Coast and Vegas at the time, then going to their home for the Christmas holidays in Colorado, so it would be after the new year before they could work me in."

Steve liked Nashville. It was cheaper and nicer than California, and the "city of music." He decided to stay in Nashville and has never regretted his decision.

"I still had some insurance money from the fire and checked into a motel but was quickly running out of money. Then I found a small guest house to rent for $300 a month.

"It was really a run-down garage with a couch that folded out to a bed, a kitchen the size of a closet, a space heater and bathroom with a free-standing metal shower." He laughed. "You could see outside light coming in at the corners of the bathroom. This was in December. And cold! Some mornings the wet floor from the night before would be frozen and I would slide into the shower."

He had a credit card, so he ordered a waterbed and because the floor was uneven, one end was a bulge of water where the water shifted.

Steve laughed. "The guy that owned the guest house also owned a shady 'pay by the hour' motel that had vibrating beds. He had leased the motel to some guys of questionable character and the landlord said he would shave $50 off my rent if I went with him to collect their rent. I dressed in a long coat and stood next to him like I had my hand on a gun. I did that once or twice.

"You do what you have to do to survive."

Steve met Joe Sullivan who was the manager with Charlie Daniels' band. Joe also managed the Winters Brothers Band, a popular Southern rock group.

"I called Joe, looking for help with an agent or manager and he gave me a job with the Winters Brothers. I only played two concerts with them. I didn't care for that style of music.

"Then I was offered an opportunity to audition with soul singer, Dobie Gray, and got the job. I learned the material, rehearsed with Dobie and was ready to play when the former keyboard player decided to come back. Dobie figured two keyboard players would be better than one keyboard player and a sax, so I never played the first gig with him.

"By now, I was feeling pretty discouraged. It was between Thanksgiving and Christmas and I kept asking myself 'what am I doing out here.' I was waiting for Donna Fargo to get back on the road and the only person I really knew was my landlord.

"I was sitting in the guest house, listening to the radio and heard 'Sand in my Shoes' by The Drifters. It got me thinking about being back at the beach. I grabbed a pen and wrote 'I've Still Got Sand in My Shoes.' I have always called it my 'Homesick Song.' I also wrote 'Carolina Man' and 'Southern Bell' while living in that shack."

Steve did not read music, but he had the melody in his head, knew what it was going to sound like. Months later, while working with Donna Fargo, Steve was introduced to the Pat Patrick Band. They played old soul and old music. Pat Patrick also owned a sound studio and was familiar with Carolina Beach music. Steve found himself telling Pat about "I've Still Got Sand in my Shoes" and his other songs.

"Let's try to record them," Pat said.

Steve sang, Pat played the piano and wrote the chords.

"He wrote them all out," Steve commented. "We did the demo of me singing and Pat on the piano. Pat said all he wanted was 50% publishing royalties and 50% writing royalties. I knew all about playing but not publishing so I agreed. Pat died a few years ago but his family still receives half of the earnings."

That New Year's Eve, Myron and the Marvells performed at the *Opryland Hotel*. They did fifties-style floor shows similar to Our House.

"After a gig I told them my background and they asked me to audition. I did and was hired immediately. They worked a lot in Florida. Ocala. Sarasota.

"The Marvells were a fun group. We did a variety of characters; one of mine was 'Turk' a football player. I would come running onto the stage in my uniform and helmet, carrying a football. As soon as I stepped up to the microphone, I'd throw the football to the bartender. One time, the bartender was talking to a customer and not paying attention to the show. I threw the ball and it went past his head, crashed into the wall of liquor bottles behind him. Almost all of the bottles shattered around him." He laughed. "Talk about making an entrance!

"I stayed with the Marvells until Donna Fargo went back on tour three months later.

Steve dressed as Turk the football player with Myron and the Marvells.

Steve performing with Myron and the Marvells. Front left, Billy Abdo, right, Michael Neel. Back left, Steve, right. Dave Shannon.

Donna Fargo

"My first job with Donna was at the Capital Center in Largo, Maryland; the next night I was in New York. Touring became extensive. I played places like Reno, Las Vegas, doing shows with people like Peter Marshall, host from Hollywood Squares. Peter Marshall also had a singing group that travelled with him. He would come out and talk about Hollywood Squares and displayed out-takes of the show that didn't pass the censors on the big screen. They were always hilarious.

"Donna Fargo had an opening act that included two elephants – Bertha and Tina They would come out on the stage where the prop crew had made a gigantic slot machine. One of Bertha's tricks was to pull the handle on the slot machine with her trunk and bananas would fall out. Somewhere, I have a picture of me sitting on Bertha's trunk.

"Another highlight was playing in California and backstage one night, I heard a familiar voice. Recognized it to be Dale Robertson, the star of the TV Show, Tales of Wells Fargo.

"Donna also suffers from Multiple Sclerosis and as the shows became more demanding, she needed to rest more. The touring dates became fewer and fewer. The band was paid by the day according to how many days they played. That was customary for a country star's back-up musician.

Much as I enjoyed travelling with her, I was having a hard time hanging on financially."

Donna Fargo and her band.
Left to right: Odell Martin, David Limerick, Terry Zimmerman, Larry
Miller, Donna Fargo, Jimmy Lowry, Steve, Darrell "BooBoo" McAfee,
Russell Easter, Gary Eichsteadt

Steve and
Donna Fargo.

Steve and Gary Ferguson, a good friend from Fredericksburg, Virginia who played guitar for Donna Fargo for a short time before leaving the group to pursue a career in bluegrass music.

Steve's first rental home in Nashville where he wrote "I've Still Got Sand in My Shoes," "Carolina Man," and "Southern Bell."

Four Guys Harmony House

When I came off the road with Donna Fargo, I moved into an apartment and a few blocks over was a supper club named *Four Guys Harmony House*. The Four Guys were a popular harmony group that played with singers such as Charlie Pride, Hank Williams, Jr, Marty Robbins and Jimmy Dean. They were long time Grand Ole Opry stars for over thirty years.

"They named the Theatre restaurant after themselves and would do two shows at the Opry then come back and do two shows at their restaurant.

"Tour buses would come to see them perform in the restaurant. I also went there a lot and got to know them, especially Sam Wellington.

"Sam knew my situation with Donna, that I was having a hard time making ends meet and had an idea. He wanted to put a DJ in the restaurant to entertain the customers while they and their band were working their Grand Old Opry spot.

"I became that DJ which now gave me a weekly salary. According to Sam, I was Nashville's first 'night club country music DJ'. I don't know if it was true, but all the other country music venues had live bands or a jukebox, so it might've been."

Steve paused. "You know, if it weren't for Sam Wellington giving me that job, I wouldn't have been able to stay in Nashville. I probably would never have had a professional career in the music business."

Dave Shannon was the light man at the restaurant. He also sang with Steve in the Marvells group.

When the *Grand Ole Opry* changed their rules and wanted the Four Guys to perform with the Opryland band, that meant the Four Guys' bandmembers were idle.

"Dave and I decided to put a vocal duo together and sang with the Four Guys Band at the restaurant while the Four Guys performed at the Opry. We called ourselves The Franklin Brothers as both our middle names were Franklin."

One night, Steve came out of the restaurant to go home and realized someone had stolen his car.

"It was a Thunderbird, less than a year old. When the cops arrived and took me home, I discovered they had also broken into my apartment. Turned out I had left a spare set of keys in the car and one of the bus boys who worked at the restaurant and knew my schedule stole it, raided my apartment, stole several pieces of sentimental jewelry, one of them being a St. Christopher's medal my step father had given me. The guy then drove to Nashville to rob a jewelry store. The store owner was there and shot the car. I ended up trading the car in because I was worried someone would recognize it and arrest me for robbery."

"One night in 1981, I met Hayward Bishop, an A-Team recording session drummer. A-Team musicians were the first recording session musicians that would get the calls to play the hits by the recording stars. They were the cream of the crop.

"During the conversation, I discovered Hayward was from Norfolk and the more we talked, we realized we both played the Virginia Beach circuit at the same time and shared an interest in soul music. He went on to play on many hit records including the early hits of Alabama, Elvis records and other well-known stars.

"Hayward was putting together a 'jam' band of studio musicians and other country acts from the South and invited me to join them.

"He had played drums on Billy Swan's hit 'I Can Help' and in return, Billy gave Hayward a song he wrote entitled, 'The Woman Needs Love.' Hayward had also built up some free studio time as musicians sometimes do in lieu of money for a session.

"We decided to go to the Castle Studio and record Billy's song and included my 'Carolina Man.' We never played the first band gig together but ended up recording 'Carolina Man' together."

Steve and Hayward decided to take the cassette to John Hook, a well-known beach music DJ in Charlotte, North Carolina to see if he would play it on the air.

"Driving from Nashville to Charlotte, we realized we didn't have a name for the band. We weren't really a band, just a group of guys and girls that would get together twice a month to play old songs they loved. Since Hayward was from Norfolk and I had played in Virginia Beach, we decided to name the band Chesapeake.

"We promoted it as 'Carolina Man' by Chesapeake and John Hook was the first DJ that played it."

I had an interesting phone interview with John Hook early one Friday morning. Beach music is his specialty and he has written fifteen books on beach and shag history. He also syndicates the *Beach Music Top 40 Countdown*, the *Roadhouse Blues, Boogie and Fish Fry, Beach Music Class Reunion* and the *Red Hot Rockabilly Show* on jukinoldies.com where he is live, Monday through Friday, 3 – 6 PM as "Fessa" John Hook.

"Steve is the second person to use the term beach music in a song," John Hook stated. "The Embers sang *about* beach music in their live concert album in 1976, but Steve specifically *says* it in his "Carolina Man – 'swingin' and a swayin' to beach music player, feels so right' – which he wrote in 1978.

"In 1981, I was broadcasting on WBT, a 50,000-watt ClearChannel station every Saturday night. On a good night, it stretched from Montreal to the Bahamas. Steve and Hayward came on the show for an interview and I played 'Carolina Man.' I thought it was terrific and started playing it on my shows. It had never been put on a record, in fact, I had the master reel to reel cassette tape and for many, many years I was the only person playing it.

"Six years later, Steve released 'I've Still Got Sand in my Shoes' and it was #1 in beach music for a number of months."

About this time, Dave Shannon left *The Four Guys Harmony House* and formed Dave Shannon and the Westside Band with three Marvell members who wanted to get off the road.

They became the house band at a club called *Amber III*.

The Club owner, Ronnie Resha, had loved the Marvells and wanted a group like that for his nightclub. When Dave had a dispute with Ronnie Resha, the band was fired.

"Those three ex-Marvell members went to Ronnie and said, 'we didn't have the falling out with you, Dave did. We want to stay. What if we find a replacement for Dave?'

"Ronnie agreed and the guys called me. I became their singer and sax player.

"Since Dave Shannon owned the group and was no longer with us, we realized we needed a new name. So, we ran a *name the band* contest. The deal was if we picked a customer's name suggestion, we would play a private party for that individual.

"Somebody submitted 'Sons of the Beach.' We thought it was a clever play on words and a name people would remember. We asked the gentleman what made him come up with the name and he said, 'The Sons of the Pioneers play western music, and you guys play a lot of beach music! Hence, Sons of the Beach.'"

The Four Guys
Left to right: Brent Burkett, Steve, Sam Wellington, Laddie Cain and John Frost.

Dave Shannon and Steve, known as Franklin Brothers.

Steve as DJ at Four Guys Harmony House

Steve and Hayward Bishop, co-founders of Chesapeake, discussing the first recording of "Carolina Man."

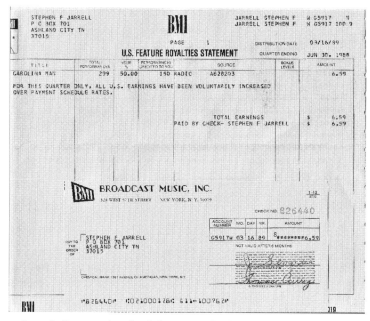

Steve's first royalty check from BMI for "Carolina Man."

Sons of the Beach

In May 1981, Steve Jarrell, Billy Abdo, Steve Patrick, Michael Neel, Jessie Gamble, and Wayne Odum became the Sons of the Beach in Nashville, Tennessee.

They were the house band at the *Amber III*, playing Carolina Beach music and oldies for five years.

"We were possibly one of the longest running house gigs in Nashville," Steve stated.

Carolina Beach music started with the rhythm and blues and soul songs of popular black recording stars in the late 1950's. Their songs featuring the horn section and happy, easy-going sounds were not played on the radios, but in the jukeboxes.

Motown and groups like The Tams, Maurice Williams and the Zodiacs and Clifford Curry brought Carolina beach music to the forefront, but it wasn't until the '80s that the beat really caught on.

As the Sons of the Beach, Steve was the lead singer and played the sax; Billy Abdo, the guitar; Steve Patrick, the keyboard; Michael Neel, drummer; Jessie Gamble, lead singer; and Wayne Odum, bass player.

They were more than a band. Steve also portrayed different characters in their floor shows.

"I'd alternate between the Duke of Earl, or wear an old ragged suit tried to do Mr. Bojangles. But there wasn't much room on the stage so I would dance on the dance floor. One night I was doing Mr. Bojangles with a cane and I forgot that the floor had a railing around. I moved across the stage and fell into the railing, bruised some ribs. Sometimes I'd wear a wig and hold a guitar to play Roy Orbison and sing 'Pretty Woman.'

"Finally, one night, I was in the back room and came out as Johnny Cadillac with my hair slicked back and an old tuxedo jacket and sunglasses. The guys didn't know about him, he just happened.

"Johnny Cadillac's mission was to make people laugh. I would splash water behind my ears and always said 'good to see ya, see ya, see ya' as I pointed to people in the audience. I always remembered Sam Wellington telling the story of how he met Billy Crash Craddock. Being an honorable man, Sam extended his hand and said 'hello' to Billy Craddock and instead of shaking Sam's hand, Billy pointed a finger at him and said, 'Crash says hi.'"

"As Johnny Cadillac, I did a rendition of 'Runaround Sue' and would brag about my *new album*, 'You've Got to Love Me Like I Do,' featuring silly made up titles."

Steve smiled. "The girls really liked Johnny Cadillac. That character stayed with me a long time.

"One lady I knew, Kim Miller, started a Fan Club! She did a quarterly newsletter, had membership cards, and gave 8x10 autographed pictures with each membership. It cost $2.79 to join and included a word find puzzle of performers' names. People actually joined! Even country star Jerry Reed.

"Years later, I took Johnny Cadillac with me to the Rock-n-Roll show at *Opryland Amusement Park* and wore a bright orange sequined jacket. That was the only jacket Opryland made for a performer in the Rock-n-Roll show.

Steve shook his head. "We had some crazy shows."

Johnny Cadillac

Johnny Cadillac in his bright orange jacket at Opryland Amusement Park.

"The *Amber III* was near Vanderbilt University. On a side street away from tourists. Celebrities often gathered there because they didn't have to worry about fans harassing them.

"Brenda Lee was one of those stars, a really sweet lady. One time, she handed me a slip of paper and said 'I can tell you're getting hoarse. I have an over the counter prescription I take.' She had written it down for me which I thought was nice.

"Rudy Gatlin of the Gatlin Brothers also came to the *Amber III*. One time I was dressed up like 'Duke of Earl,' wore a solid white suit with a ¾ length jacket, silver shirt and silver shoes. I had a cane, one of those pageboy hats and glasses that looked like venetian blinds.

"Rudy loved those shoes so much he bought them off my feet for a hundred dollars.

"Famous songwriter Mack Vickery was another frequent visitor. Remember 'Jamestown Ferry'? He also wrote 'I'm the Only Hell My Mama Ever Raised' which was a big hit. Mack was also good friends with Jerry Lee Lewis and wrote many of Jerry Lee Lewis' songs.

"Mack lived in the same apartment complex as me and we became friends. This was around the time infomercials selling albums on TV became popular. Mack wanted to do one and asked me to sing background."

Steve laughed.

"He was going to name it 'Mack Vickery's Greatest Hits, Vol. 2.' I asked Mack about the first volume, said I'd like to have a copy. He replied there wasn't one. He figured if he titled it volume two, everyone would think the first was sold out!"

Mack often invited Jerry Lee Lewis to come to see Steve at *Amber III*.

"One night I sang 'My Prayer' by the Platters and Jerry Lee complimented me on it. He said 'only two people can really sing that song. Tony Williams and you.'"

Another night, Steve invited Jerry Lee Lewis to come on stage and play with the band.

"They had just done one of those TV shows – I think it was '60 Minutes' – about his three wives that had died."

Steve shook his head.

"Jerry Lee Lewis got on the stage and said, 'I guess you saw me on TV. It hurt my feelings. The only person ole' Jerry Lee tried to kill was himself.'

"Then he started playing 'Born to Lose' with the band and I didn't know WHAT to think.

"But he was always pleasant and friendly. One day he bought a new car and brought it by the *Amber III* for me to see it. He didn't know how to use half of the gadgets that were loaded on it."

An *ABC Movie of the Week* MY BODY MY CHILD, starring Vanessa Redgrave and Joe Campanella was filmed in Nashville.

"The cast and crew stayed across the street and about a block away from *Amber III* and would come the Club to relax. They always had a good time and as a result, the producers wrote a scene of Vanessa and Ed together at the Club with Sons of the Beach in the background.

"They made this big sign with our name on it, decorated the stage with fish-net and a captain's wheel which they gave to me."

This explained to me why Steve would have a captain's wheel on a wall in his office.

"Then there was Charlie McAlexander, a sports caster for Channel 4 – WSMV TV in Nashville. He also liked to sing. He was on the *Noon Show,* a daily program on Channel 4 and would sing every other week with the Sons of Beach backing him up.

"Wayne Odum and I wrote an original song the band recorded called '4 – the Love of Summer.' The station liked it and made a TV commercial with the Sons of the Beach performing with the TV anchors.

"That commercial ran all summer long. We were never paid but the promotion was fantastic. A clothing store provided our outfits for each show and that's how I acquired an assortment of multi-colored pants and IZOD shirts.

"Girls would come to the *Amber III,* sit at tables and listen to us play. During breaks, the guys in the band would meander the crowd and socialize with the people. Back then I guess you'd say I was shy and didn't talk too much with the girls."

But one beautiful blonde at one of those tables caught Steve's eye. He also noticed she didn't socialize or dance much either.

"Barry Sullivan, a friend from Fredericksburg who was single at the time was visiting, and he started up a conversation with her. Barry came back to me and said, 'you ought to meet this girl.'"

That's how Steve met Cindy Nelson from Chattanooga, Tennessee, the lady who would become his wife.

"My work is having a company dinner and I'd like you to come," Cindy said one night.

"I would love to," Steve replied, "but I have to work."

Cindy sighed. "How do you like that. The first time I ask a guy out and he turns me down."

"I felt bad but said I would make it up to her. I asked if I could take her to see Myron and the Marvells at the *Opryland Hotel*. She accepted. We started dating and got married a year later."

Steve and Cindy bought a house on the Cumberland River in Ashland City, twelve miles outside Nashville. "It was a little cottage with a boat dock; we really liked that house. We had an English sheepdog named 'BoBo' and our daughter Austin Leigh was born while we lived there."

133

In addition to playing with the Sons of the Beach, Billy Abdo and Wayne Odum did an Oldies Show at *Opryland Amusement Park*. Their sax player left the group, so Billy asked Steve to join the band.

"I sang and performed as Johnny Cadillac at the Amusement Park during the day for four hours then played with the Sons of the Beach nights, nine to one in the morning at *Amber III*. I did this for three years."

Opryland Amusement Park was seasonal so during the winter of 1983, Steve looked elsewhere to support his family and got into radio announcing.

Steve paused.

"Do you remember that record 'Mr. Magic Man' and 'Up on the Roof' that Our House did in 1973? Well, Stan Hardin, the guy that wrote it, decided to release the record about this time. Ten years after we recorded it. 'Up on the Roof' caught the attention of the beach music radio stations when they flipped the record over.

"It was promoted as 'Bob Speck and Our House featuring Steve Jarrell' and began getting airplay. At the second Beach Music Awards show, 'Up on the Roof' was nominated for single of the year and I was nominated Male Vocalist of the Year. Lou Rawls was also nominated and won.

"Doc Damon was another radio announcer at a top rock station in town and he and I did a weekly TV afternoon show on Viacom called *Let's Go Rock 'n' Roll*. It was a local version of *American Bandstand* and we invited different schools each week to dance. We hired recording stars like Ronnie Dove, Gene Simmons, and other guest stars around town to appear on the show.

"Doc and I were also hired by CMT – *Country Music Television* – in the company's earlier days to appear in different music videos. We would wear fake getups like wigs, mustaches, etc. so we could do several of the videos.

"Some other music videos we performed in that come to mind are 'Hey Bartender' by Johnny Lee; 'You've Really Got a Hold on Me' by Mikey Gilley; 'Another Drinking Song' by Johnny Nail; 'So Good' by Thrasher Brothers; and Alan Jackson's 'Pop A Top Again.'"

The music videos led to other opportunities in television. Steve hosted a movie show called *Night Owl Theater* as Johnny Cadillac on Channel 2 and did comedy skits and characters on DJ Coyote McCloud's local segments of *Elvira's Movie Macabre* on Channel 17.

"The TV show *Dukes of Hazzard* was popular at this time and I did two commercials dressed as Boss Hogg on Channel 5.

"At one point, I was on NBC, ABC, CBS, FOX and Viacom all at the same time doing different things from comedy characters to commercials. I'm also performing with the Sons of the Beach at *Amber III* and working what seemed like twenty-four hours each day."

The movies were still coming to town, so Steve started a side business – *Star Car Classics*. He ran ads in *Wheels and Deals* magazine looking for vintage cars to be used in movies and television.

"I had a rolodex of classic car owners interested in loaning their cars for videos and movies. I had met the head of the Tennessee Film Commission who added my name to the Film Commission directory.

"Tri-Star Pictures started filming SWEET DREAMS. It was about Patsy Cline and stared Jessica Lange and Ed Harris. Walt Freitas was the movie's transportation manager. He found my name in the Directory and called to say he needed fifteen to thirty-five cars each day. Car owners would drop their car off, give me the keys and the teamsters would drive the car in the film. Then the owners came back to pick it up in the evening.

"Freitas paid me $100 per car and I made ten percent on the deals. I did this for another movie – MARIE – staring Cissy Spacek."

Then Steve heard the SWEET DREAMS director, Karel Reisz, was auditioning for a band to be in the movie backing Jessica Lange at the demolition derby scene.

"Several sax players auditioned. I knew during that era, the sax player didn't just stand there and play so I added some steps, threw the horn in the air and got the job.

Steve performing with Jessica Lange in SWEET DREAMS.

Steve and Ed Harris on set of SWEET DREAMS

The Sons of the Beach play soul music hits from the '60s and '70s tonight and tomorrow at Amber lii, 106 29th Ave. N. No cover charge.

The original members of the Sons of the Beach.
Top row: Steve Patrick, Steve Jarrell, Michael Neel. Bottom row: Jesse Gamble, Wayne Odum, Billy Abdo. Wayne left and Terry Dunn took his place.

First Sons of the Beach
Top Row, left to right: Michael Neal, Steve Patrick, Jesse Gamble.
Bottom row, Steve, Billy Abdo, Terry Dunn.

Backdrop for the Sons of the Beach performance in the movie
MY BODY MY CHILD.

Steve and the Sons of the Beach with Charlie McAlexander on
the Channel 4 Noon Show.

Steve and Catherine "Daisy Duke" Bach from Dukes of Hazzard.

"Boss Hogg" Steve with the guys filming Dukes of Hazzard commercials.

Steve, Mickey Gilley and Bob Speck doing "You've Really Got a Hold On Me" music video.

Steve, Charles Esten of "Nashville" series and Doug Bell of Belleview Cadillac.

Casper Van Dien and Steve after filming movie 11 SECONDS renamed ACQUITTED BY FAITH.

July 4, 1984

One night in 1983, Steve was riding along Briley Parkway and heard Les Jamison on the radio interviewing Pete Bennett, the promotion man for the Beatles. He also had Joe Rannellucci and Walt Davison from Philadelphia on the show. All three of the men were in town to promote a wax museum for the Beatles.

Pete Bennett said, "I've made unknowns into stars and stars into superstars. Superstars are known by their first names – Elvis, Cher, Beatles."

Steve decided this was a guy he wanted to meet.

"This was before cell phones, so I pulled off the parkway, parked at a gas station near a phone booth and listened to the rest of the interview. When it was over, I called the station, asked to speak to Pete Bennett.

"They said he was leaving but I persisted and said it was only for a minute. They put him on the phone, and I asked, if he had heard of beach music, particularly East Coast Carolina Beach Music. He said he hadn't.

"Can I have fifteen minutes to show you something?" I asked.

"Pete Bennett invited me to *Spence Manor* where he was staying."

Steve went to his apartment, packed up all his beach music magazines, cassettes, anything else he could find pertaining to Carolina beach music. Drove to *Spence Manor* and for two hours, wowed Pete Bennett with his sizeable memorabilia collection.

"Man!" Bennett exclaimed, "I've been in the music business fifty years and in comes a guy showing me something I've never heard of before, Carolina beach music! Never seen this much."

Pete Bennett, Joe Rannellucci and Walt Davison started coming to *Amber III* to hear Steve and the Sons of the Beach.

"I want to do something for you guys," Walt Davison said. "Don't know when, but I want to do something."

Steve said sure but didn't put much faith in the statement. People were always saying that.

Six months later, Steve got a call.

"This is Walt Davison. Remember me? I didn't have anything at the time but now I do. How would you like to play with the Beach Boys on their 4th of July Celebration in Philadelphia?"

"We'll walk if we have to," I said. "It ended up our local Budweiser Beer distributor bought our airline tickets."

"Beach Boys Bring on the Summer" turned out to be the largest concert ever. Six and a half hours of music that included the Oak Ridge Boys, Christopher Cross, Robert Hazard, Joe Ely, Neville Brothers, Frank Stallone, Katrina & The Waves, Jimmy Page from Led Zeppelin, Joan Jett and the Blackhearts.

And the Sons of the Beach.

This was Mike Love's charity event to raise money for the Love Foundation that campaigned against world hunger. They were also donating to the renovation of the Statue of Liberty.

By then, Dennis Wilson had died but every year the Beach Boys would feature a guest drummer. This year, Ringo Starr was supposed to be there, and Steve was excited to finally meet one of the Beatles. But Ringo had to cancel at the last minute because his mother in England was sick.

"You'll never believe who they got to replace Ringo. Mr. T! I didn't even know he played drums! He was there in this big tee-shirt covering up all his jewelry."

All the musicians rode limos down the Ben Franklin Parkway to the stage.

"We were waiting inside a limo when Joan Jett – Queen of Rock 'n' Roll and Godmother of Punk jumped in. She was pretty cool. We were in the back laughing and talking with her, until her manager got in. He looked over at us."

"Who are you guys?" He demanded.

"Sons of the Beach, we have one record," I answered.

The manager started hollering at Joan, "get out of the car! You can't ride with them, they are nobodies."

Steve chuckled. "He made her get out! She was embarrassed about it.

"The setting for the concert was amazing. There were these huge monstrous tents as backdrops; the stage was way up, so high we were looking down on the inflatable tops of the beer cans. It was held off Ben Franklin Parkway, in front of the steps of the Philadelphia Art Museum where Sylvester Stallone ran up the steps in the movie ROCKY. They had to shut down the Parkway which was full of people.

"There was a monster PA system and half-way down the parkway there was another sound system.

"The concert drew one-point-two million making it the largest concert at the time. The place was packed! People had large coolers of beer and sodas; the Parkway was like a backyard tailgate party. People were barbequing hamburgers and chickens, stretched out on blankets. They set off firecrackers, threw frisbees and footballs and drank beer. Some of the guys were climbing the trees and light poles to get a better view.

"Behind the stage, they had this huge chain-link fence around the area for the entertainers. Dressing room trailers were parked in a circle around a big tent in the center with food and refreshments for the entertainers to hang out and relax.

"I remember kids hollering to Mr. T. And he was hollering back 'buy My Cereal'. I think he was doing some promotion at the time and had his picture on boxes of cereal.

"One guy with a British accent came up and grabbed the sleeve of my Hawaii shirt."

"I thought I was the only one that wore these."

"He walked off and I just looked at him, wondered who in the world is that guy?"

"You don't know that guy!" Somebody said. "That was Jimmy Page from Led Zeppelin."

"It was an amazing day. And the next day, we were back in *Opryland Amusement Park* playing a gig."

Mike Love, Steve and Bruce Johnston, 2018.

Bruce Johnston of "Beach Boys," Joan Jett and Steve at July 4th Concert.

Richard Sterban (Oak RIdge Boys) at July 4th Concert.

.

Benefits, Floods and Fire #2

With a wife and child to support, Steve would do anything to make a buck during the off season at *Opryland Amusement Park.* He was still singing with Sons of the Beach nights but worked other jobs during the day.

For a short time, he worked as a booking agent for Maxcy-Patrick Talent Agency. Pat Patrick had a crew called Pat Patrick Band and was familiar with beach music. The agency became Prime Source Entertainment started by Lee Maxcy who was Steve's agent for more than 30 years and still is today.

Steve also worked with S&J Productions.

"This was around the time K-Tel records started reproducing recordings of original artists for national distribution. They did not have the original masters, so they hired S&J to reproduce the background music then hired the original singers to come in to re-cut the record.

"My job was to locate the artists and negotiate the contract for which I made a ten-percent commission. I also met and transported the singers from the airport to *Spence Manor* where they stayed, then to the studio and back to the airport.

"I worked with lots of stars, one being Spanky and Our Gang's Elaine McFarland. She not only did the Spanky songs, but she also sang with the Mama's and Papa's. Mama Cass had died, and Elaine McFarland sounded almost like her. So, she did Mama Cass's part for K-Tel and ended up joining the band.

"Jay Black, lead singer for Jay and The Americans was interesting. I tracked him to a club in New York City. I would call the club and they would transfer me to his dressing room. Did that several times, and every time, he would hang up on me. Finally, he answered, and I booked him to come and record. When he got to Nashville and I picked him up at the airport, I asked why he kept hanging up on me. He said he was going through a divorce and thought I was his wife's attorney.

"Dennis Tufano, lead singer with The Buckinghams came a day early so I invited him to *Amber III* to hear the Sons of the Beach. When Dennis did the session the next day, he commented, 'you sound like Nick' – the other Buckingham. He asked me to sing in the background. We got to be friends, did several other gigs together.

"Back in the Rotations days at the *Peabody's Warehouse* in Virginia Beach, we did a show with the Kingsmen of 'Louie, Louie' fame. Remember, that was the night they came to the party at the band house and we were kicked out. The bass player was a guy named Jeff Beals.

"Jeff ended up in Nashville working for the William Morris Talent Agency. He booked major name acts for the agency and remembered doing the show with us at *Peabody's* in 1968. We also became friends. Jeff was a terrific bari sax player and would come and play with us sometimes.

"Jeff would have jam sessions at his house when some of the name acts came to town and he often invited me to join them.

"At one of those sessions I met Max Weinberg – Bruce Springsteen's drummer. He later became the band leader on the Conan O'Brian show and whenever I went to New York, I went to the Conan O'Brian show and would hang out backstage. That's how I met newsman Tom Brokaw and actress Tina Fey."

In 1985, Steve participated in a benefit for John Richbourg, an American disc jockey known as John R.

"John R played rhythm and blues music on Nashville radio, WLAC. He was also a record producer and artist manager.

"He was called the Hitmaker because he and Bill "Hoss Man" Allen were on the radio late at night and would play newcomers. They were responsible for a lot of rhythm and blues singers being heard. Guys like Chuck Berry, Fats Domino, James Brown and Otis Redding became successful because of them.

"They had sponsors for their show, and you could order through them; they sold records, even chickens!

"John R died in 1986 but on March 25, 1985, a benefit concert was held at the *Ryman* to help pay for some of his steep medical bills.

"James Brown gave one of the best performances of his career there. It was a two-day affair and the Sons of the Beach were hired to perform at the banquet the night before. The Neville Brothers, Charlie Daniels, James Brown, The Coasters and more performed the next day. Wolfman Jack, BB King, all the guys John R helped were there and I got to meet them all. It was amazing."

Steve and John R.
"The Hitmaker"

Program for the benefit for
John R. "The Hitmaker"

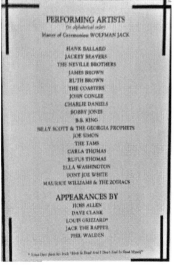

Steve, Rufus Thomas and B.B. King at the John R. Benefit.

Maurice Williams and Steve at the John R. Benefit.

Hoss Man Allen and Steve at the John R. Benefit.

Steve had all this going in addition to playing at *Opryland Amusement Park.* One day, a storm came up, the park started flooding and shows were shut down. "Somebody approached me and said I needed to go home to Ashland City.

"Your house is flooded. Cindy and Austin are okay, but they had to leave the dog behind."

Steve rushed home, checked on Cindy and Austin who were staying with her mother. They had been rescued in a boat but had to leave BoBo behind because they worried his excitement would tip the boat over. The next day Steve went to look at the house and arrived just as a TV guy was going out to check on the flooding.

"I asked if I could ride along. Explained that my dog was still missing. We had a four-foot high chain link fence around the property and only six inches of the fence was showing. There were snakes in the water, it was awful. We rode around the house but found no signs of BoBo. Then as we were pulling away, I heard a bark. BoBo had somehow gotten up on some steps and had been holding his head above the water all night.

"We lived in a house trailer while having the house rebuilt. Replaced all the appliances and moved back in around Thanksgiving.

"I had come home to Fredericksburg to perform in the *Turkey Trot* at the Sheraton for the Jaycees. I did this for several years."

He left a day early, planning to stay with his friend Barry Sullivan.

"This was before cell phones, so I was surprised when Barry asked if I'd like a beer then told me to have a seat as soon as I walked in the door."

"First," Barry said, "Cindy and Austin are okay, but your house has burned down."

Cindy had a small consignment business with children's clothes called Austin's Attic. She and Austin left to go to the shop and fifteen minutes later the brand new *HotPoint* refrigerator exploded, blew out the back windows and burned the house down.

This had happened to another family in North Carolina and the insurance company would not let Steve sue the company because they were in the process themselves.

Charles Weimer, one of Steve's friends, owned *Arbuckle's* restaurant at the time and he and the Jaycees sponsored a drive for clothes, toys, household goods and donations.

Days later, Steve got a call from the manager of the *Holiday Inn North* in Fredericksburg asking him to come back to Virginia, put the band together and get the club going again. The property was owned by a company in Norfolk and as the entertainment director, Steve would get the Fredericksburg site straight, then work with the other properties around the state.

Steve discussed this with Cindy who replied, "you've always wanted to move back to Fredericksburg. Now's the time to do it. We don't have anything to move."

They found a house at Fairview Beach that was owner financed, requiring a $10,000 down payment which just happened to equal the settlement from the fire.

Steve then started a local Sons of Beach with Larry Haywood, Ronny Baker, Chris Epolito, and Jon Buda. keyboard player.

Everything went smoothly until the week before the club was to open.

"I got a call from the manager who said he had bad news. The parent company had decided not to go with live entertainment.

"Suddenly I was in a bad situation. I had a mortgage, bills to pay and no job. Many of my friends came to the rescue. Kenny and Sonja Gallahan owned *King George Video* and gave me a job working evenings in the video store. Bran Dillard owner of *Picker's Supply* gave me a job at the music store."

Then Chris Hallberg, another high school classmate, called him.

"Chris had bought Sullivan Lumber Yard and wanted to sell off as much as he could before the auction. He needed somebody to take care of it and offered to pay me $300 a week to watch the place.

"I was supposed to start the following Monday, but the Thursday or Friday before, I went to a market in Fairview Beach; stepped of the curb, tripped and broke my foot. I had to start work with a cast. On the third day, we were loading concrete on a truck and a bag fell off. It burst and spilled concrete into my cast. It started burning my leg and I sawed the cast off with a hacksaw. I had to let the foot heal itself."

Steve sighed heavily. "We were struggling. Cindy's working two jobs, I'm working two jobs, doing what I needed to do. Talk about humility.

"Since we had put the band together, we played wherever we could. Fairview Beach, Fredericksburg, anywhere. Charles Weimer hired us at *Arbuckle's,* but it was hard to make ends meet. I was making two, three hundred dollars a night but that had to be split with the band."

In November 1986, Steve got a call from Don Denbo who used to come to the *Amber III.*

"I know you don't remember me, but I came into the *Amber III* with some buddies. I'd have a few beers then get up on the stage with you."

Steve knew exactly who Don Denbo was because he always sang The Showmen's song, "39-21-46" and not many people knew that song.

After getting reacquainted, Don explained the reason for his call. "Randy Davidson, the owner of Central South Record Distributors and I are the principal owners of the *Treasure Island Resort* in the Cayman Islands and we want the Sons of the Beach to come down there and play."

The resort was also owned by eight country music stars – Conway Twitty, Gatlin Brothers, Ronnie Milsap, Earl Thomas Conley, Dave Rowland, Helen Cornelius, Deborah Allen and Jerry Reed.

"With all those stars, why don't you want a country house band?" I asked.

"We want the same fun atmosphere that the Sons of the Beach presented at the *Amber III* in Nashville," Don replied.

"Well, I'm in Virginia and don't have that same group together anymore."

"Find out what it will take to put the band back together and get back to me," Don suggested.

Steve called all the guys – Billy Abdo, David Limerick, Rob Lau, Marshall Pearson, Paul Lamoureux – and asked what each wanted. Explained that everything was tax free.

"We figured nothing ventured, nothing gained. I totaled what everyone wanted, added what I wanted and told Don, here's what it's going to cost."

"You've got it!" Don answered.

Cayman Islands

Steve returned to Nashville two weeks before they were to leave for the Caymans to rehearse with the band. Four of the bandmembers had worked together – David Limerick, Paul Lamoureaux, Billy Abdo and me – but two, Rob Lau and Marshall Pearson were new.

"Rob came over from a '50s group The Vandells and Marshall had been Roy Orbison's drummer.

"We had all worked with floor shows in the past and pulled from those experiences to create new ones.

"We also decided we needed a put together an album to sell to the tourists and in two days, we recorded CAYMAN VACATION. I designed the cover to look like a scrapbook page. You know, with those black glue-backed tabs at each corner of the pictures.

"That album was never released in the U.S. We produced a limited number and sold it only in the Caymans. I've been asked a couple times to release it again but never have.

"When we got to the Islands, I visited some of the businesses and recruited six to be sponsors at $500 each. Then I took pictures of the six of us at the businesses. Robbie was on a jet ski; David was at the airport; Marshall on a scooter; Paul was at a Black Coral jewelry store; Billy was at a restaurant and I was in front of a rental car. We put the business name and phone number beneath the picture on the cover.

"There was a really popular guy on the islands. His name was George Nowak, but everyone called him Barefoot Man. He was an American musician that moved to the islands long before the immigration laws and as a result was grandfathered in as a citizen. He had played for different artists but at the time didn't have a job. One New Year's Eve he filled in at a hotel where the band they had hired didn't show up and he ended up being the regular entertainer.

"George is the best kept secret in the music business. He did albums and cassettes wrote songs as well as books. He still does. He wrote a coffee table book called *The People Time Forgot: A Photographic Portrayal of the people at Cayman Islands*.

"He was the King of the Island and everybody thought the Sons of the Beach, being the new kids in town, would be competition. I called him and asked if he would distribute our records and tapes, and we would pay him a percentage. We ended up becoming friends."

The two principal owners of the *Treasure Island Resort* were Don Denbo and Randy Davidson.

"Don was an insurance man who underwrote policies for the world wrestling federation as well as Ringling Brothers. Randy owned Central South Music, one of the largest record distributors. This was before CD's.

"Don and Randy didn't know much about the hotel business. The *Paradise Manor Resort* had been partially built, then abandoned. Don and Randy came in and finished it. Holly Powers from Boston played a big part in the success of the resort. Her profession was tourism and she brought large tour groups to stay there when it first opened.

"I've always admired Holly for her accomplishments. I ran into her again in the '90s when I was playing at the Hyatt in Hilton Head. By coincidence, she had a group of tourists there too. We caught up and she began booking the Sons of the

Beach. Took us to Cancun, Bermuda, and other shows. She was largely responsible for our international performances.

"One time, she booked us in Bermuda for an employee appreciation party given by *Jordan's Furniture* in the Boston area. The company flew all their employees to Bermuda for a beach party for the day. It was considered the largest employee party ever. We were hired to play and got a lot of press with that performance."

The eight country music stars that invested in the *Treasure Island Resort* would often visit the islands to relax and sometimes perform. Being the house band, Steve and the Sons of the Beach would usually perform an hour before the artists or back them up if their band wasn't there.

"It was a good life. With so many country music stars involved, there was a lot of worldwide press and the Sons of the Beach were often mentioned.

"We often went parasailing on the boats with the stars. I even became a certified scuba diver and worked with another scuba diver to film a YouTube of me playing my sax under water. I called it Aqua Sax.

"Ian Gillan with Deep Purple who sang 'Smoke on Water' was there with his wife, Braun and daughter, Gracie who was about the same age as Austin. The kids played in the pool together.

"I introduced Ian to Conway Twitty. One night, Ian came in and I went over to say hi. We chatted and I asked if he would like to sit in with the band. He was apprehensive, said he had never performed with anyone other than his own band.

"We'll rehearse with you," I said.

"You will? I'll need a harmonica."

"I'll take you to a music store, get you one."

Steve grinned. "And we did. I even told him it was nice to know he was an average guy. We are still friends to this day.

He and his wife flew over to Nashville a few years back and stayed ten days in Springfield, Tennessee with me.

"Funny story here. When Ian and Braun came to Springfield only two people recognized him. One night we went to Nashville just to walk around. They were having the grand opening of the *Hard Rock Café* that night. We walked by and I said to Ian, 'let's go inside.'"

"Okay, they have some of my memorabilia in there."

When they started inside, the security guard stopped them. "I'm sorry, this is a private event for VIP's only."

"I leaned over to Ian and said, 'let me tell him who you are.'"

"No Mate," Ian said with a smile and kept walking.

"If only that security guard knew," Steve chortled. "And if the management knew, he would probably have lost his job, knowing that the guard had just turned away one of the biggest rock stars in the world. But in the security guard's defense, Ian had his long flowing hair pulled back into a tight bun on the back of his head. And wore a cardigan sweater."

Steve has always been an early riser and was out walking the Cayman beaches one morning when he saw Johnny and June Cash. They were flying to their home in Jamaica and had stayed overnight at the resort. They were coming out of their condo on their way to the airport.

"I'm about to starve to death," Steve heard June comment.

"Excuse me, my condo is right here. I'll be glad to make you a sandwich." He made them sandwiches and escorted them to the cab to leave for their flight.

"Before you leave, can I get a picture?" Steve asked

They said sure!

"There was always a lot to do on the Caymans but not a lot to do if you know what I mean. We would always take two or three days each week to rehearse the challenging songs like 'Good Vibrations' and Richard Harris' 'McArthur Park.' It took me a week to learn that one."

Steve remembered working on a model car kit.

"I had paint on my hands and met this lady nicknamed 'Snick.' She noticed my hands and said her husband was a hobbyist as well. He liked trains and she went on to say he had found a rail car. I figured they kept it in their back yard. Then she showed me a picture of a real working train car from out West with the glass dome roof for viewing!

"She said every year the family got together in Chicago and hooked it to another rail car and travelled across country." He laughed. "I guess they must have paid by the mile to do that.

"Come to find out, her daughter was married to Tony Butala, leader of the Lettermen. You just never knew who you were going to meet down there. We're still friends today."

Conway Twitty was taping his *Silver Eagle* radio show and decided to record it at the resort. As usual the Sons of the Beach played a set before the star came out and did his show.

"Conway worked with the Kaminski Sound Co. who also worked with Paul Simon. An hour before the show was due to start, everyone was set up, waiting for Conway. The engineer came up to me."

"Do you want to cut a live album? We're already set up. It won't cost you anything. You'll only have one shot though."

"I'd been holding 'I've Still Got Sand in My Shoes,' 'Carolina Man' and 'Southern Belle' since 1979 and finally I had a chance to record them. In fact, whenever I play 'I've Still Got Sand in my Shoes' on a radio show, I use that recording.

"We met all kinds of interesting people in the Caymans. Some had lots of money and we learned not to ask where their money came from. One guy always gave big tips and we could tell whenever he was in town because he would send a bottle of Dom Perignon Champagne to the band whenever he was there."

TNN – The Nashville Network – did a week-long *Nashville Now* broadcast down there, interviewing artists. Steve got to meet Mike Love again, Cory Wells of Three Dog Night and Brian Hyland.

"Remember I'd met Brian in the '60s when he and the Prophets played on the *Good Guys Show* at James Madison High School in Brooklyn. I remembered being starry-eyed and excited to meet him. After the show, I said, 'good show, Brian' and he just looked at me and said, 'the worst'.

"Needless to say, I didn't have a good impression after that.

"Fast forward twenty years and Brian had come to the Caymans with his ten-year-old son Brodie. Most of the people didn't know who Brian was, so I helped to get them situated. Offered to show them around the island, took them to the Turtle farm which was a popular venue.

"You don't remember me," I said on the way to the Turtle farm, "but when I first met you, here's what happened."

After explaining the story, Steve said, "It's nice to know you get a second chance to make a first impression. We became friends after that."

The Islands were a great time for the family as well. Stephen Franklin Jarrell, Jr. was born in Georgetown Hospital in the Caymans on December 21, 1987. Austin was four years old and started school there, wore the school uniforms. She took ballet, even performed in a show for the Governor.

The people were friendly and Steve, Cindy and the kids were accepted into the community, attended get-togethers, and knew most of the businesses.

There was a governmental agency called the Protection Board that managed everything on the island with exception of the tourists. Everything had to go through the Protection Board.

Many of the local musicians were upset when the Sons of the Beach moved down there and had formed their own musician's union. Barefoot Man was grandfathered into the union, he had been there for so long.

Steve shook his head. "I tried to join and abide by the rules, but they wouldn't let me. They wanted equal time in the hotel and equal money. The resort said they couldn't afford it. Would have to cut nights back for the band."

The Sons of the Beach ended up leaving the Caymans after two years. The resort tried other bands but eventually shut down. The local bands took over but never succeeded.

"When the party was over, everybody came home. Rob Lau the keyboard player decided to stay and worked with the local musicians. The rest of us returned to Nashville.

The six guys in that combination of the Sons of the Beach never performed together in the U.S. We did gigs in the Bahamas, Bermuda and Cancun, Mexico but never the U.S.

Arial view of the Treasure Island Resort

Cayman Island Sons of the Beach
Left to right: Marshall Pearson, David Limerick, Paul Lamoureaux, Billy Abdo, Steve, Rob Lau.

Nashville Now in the Cayman Islands.
T.G. Sheppard, Randy Travis, Gene Watson, Mike Love
and the Sons of the Beach, Steve........

Ian Gillan and Steve in the Cayman Islands.

Steve and
Ian Gillan in
2015.

Ian Gillan performing with Steve and the Sons of the Beach.

Johnny Cash, June Carter Cash and Steve.

Steve and Brian Hyland

Sons of the Beach beside the pool in the Cayman Islands
Standing, left to right: Rob Lau, Steve, Marshall Pearson, David
Limerick. Seated, Paul Lamoureux and Billy Abdo in chair.

Cayman Vacation Album.

Nashville

After the Caymans, Steve and the family returned to Fairview Beach, Virginia. The rest of the guys went to Nashville.

The Sons of the Beach and "I've Still Got Sand In My Shoes" became popular in beach music, and Steve found himself commuting to Nashville on weekends to perform. He decided to buy a tour bus which he admits was a big mistake.

"Talk about going broke!"

He missed little Stevie's first birthday party because they had problems with the clutch on their way to a gig in Huntington, West Virginia and it broke down.

"We made the gig, but the bus had to be towed."

Marshall Pearson shared another event on the tour bus. "One time, we took a job near Memphis where we had to park in a field. They had mowed a path for us like a road. We drove in and followed the path with no problem. Then it rained and it was like a flood came through, made for a soggy field. When it came time to leave, we couldn't see the path, just headed across the field and got stuck. Suddenly, the bus was in mud up to the axels. It took two wreckers with 100-foot cables to pull it out. One of the cables snapped but we eventually got out.

"A musician's life isn't easy," Marshall continued. "My definition of a musician is the guy that packs $5000 of equipment into a $500 van, drives 500 miles to make $50 an hour. It was feast or famine, had its ups and downs but we survived. It's the most amazing time and worth it when you're on stage."

The band went through some personnel changes. "We wanted to keep as many together as we could but one by one, they left except Marshall Pearson, the drummer, who is still with with me. Bill Abdo moved to Scottsdale, Arizona; Paul returned to Canada; David went back to Fredericksburg.

"I even left the group a couple times. But by 1990 we finally got everything straight and they are still with me now with exception of one."

Steve and the Band's popularity had grown not only from the success of "I've Still Got Sand in My Shoes" but the press received from being in the Caymans with all the stars. Things were happening like other appearances on TNN's Nashville Now, a Ronnie Milsap special with the Sons of the Beach, The Crickets, and Fabian as well as Ronnie and other appearances. So, Steve, Cindy and the kids made the decision to return to Nashville for good.

"Here in Nashville, music is a business. It's the theme of the city. If you buy a house here and list musician as your job, it is accepted. Anywhere else, the banker will say, what's your real job?

"With Nashville being the center of the music industry, I was around musicians all the time which is what I loved. They shared my passion and there were more opportunities."

Steve paused. "There are so many components to Nashville, maybe I need to give you a little background on the city.

"First, there's the *Ryman* which was built by Thomas Ryman as the *Union Gospel Tabernacle* in 1892 to serve large scale revivals. The name was changed to *Ryman* when he died in 1904.

"In addition to revivals, the facility was leased to speakers, entertainers, concerts, even boxing matches to pay off some of the construction debt.

"Then, in the late 1940's, country music stars began performing there regularly. The country music radio program, *Grand Ole Opry*, was broadcasted in several venues around Nashville but in 1943, it was done at the *Ryman* where it remained for the next thirty-one years. It was so popular people were turned away from sold out shows.

"In 1963, WSM Radio purchased the building and named it the *Grand Ole Opry House*. By then, the building was beginning to deteriorate so they decided to build a new venue and in 1969 they purchased a large tract of land on Briley Parkway outside Nashville.

"This was next to *Opryland Amusement Park* that was already under construction and opened in March, 1972. The park operated March through October and became a popular tourist attraction. Rides were offered, but the theme of the park was American music with shows.

"Two years later, in 1974, the *Grand Ole Opry House* had their first show in the brand-new facility and offered shows two days each week. Being adjacent to the Amusement Park, there was a plaza at the main entrance.

"In 1977, a large hotel and Convention center was constructed next door to the Opry House. It has since been named the *Gaylord Opryland Resort and Convention Center*.

"The music shows at the amusement park were so popular, they decided to build a small theater next to the Opry House for premiere shows and named it the *Acuff Theater* after Roy Acuff the King of Country music.

"In 1983, Gaylord Broadcasting Company of Oklahoma City, now the Gaylord Entertainment Company, purchased the entire Opryland project. TNN the Nashville Television Network broadcasted 'Nashville Now' live from the Gaslight Theater inside the park and big-name country stars began hosting concerts there.

"Business was good until 1997 when *Opryland Amusement Park* closed its doors. But the *Grand Ole Opry*, *Acuff Theater* and *Gaylord Opryland Resort* were still there.

"On May 1, 2010, torrential rains flooded the *Grand Ole Opry* and the stage was submerged under ten feet of water. But that didn't stop the show. They moved it to the *Municipal Auditorium* in the city until the twenty-million-dollar renovation was completed four months later.

"So," Steve exhaled, "that gives you a little background of the city I love. You'll see that all of those venues have played a part in my life."

When Steve and Cindy moved back to Tennessee in 1989, they found a house in Springfield, twenty-five minutes outside Nashville.

"Ashland City was too small; Nashville was too big. When I was on the radio years earlier, I went to Springfield for an event and it reminded me of Fredericksburg."

Steve continued to play with the Sons of the Beach but returned to radio shortly after moving to Springfield.

The following year, Steve took a six-month hiatus from the band and radio to come to Fredericksburg to help Tommy Mitchell with the Colonial Theater.

"Clifford Curry didn't have a band, so the Sons of the Beach worked with him while I was gone.

"Tommy Mitchell wanted to turn the Colonial Theater, an old movie theater, into a Performing Arts Center and have bands perform there.

"I was involved in the transition, set up the PA system and lighting; booked the acts and pretty much managed the property. The primary focus was to have live musical acts and we had fourteen shows, ten of them with national recording stars. Stars like Country Gentlemen, Gary Lewis and Playboys, The Impressions, Bill Deal and the Rhondels, Leon Redbone and Pirates of the Mississippi just to name a few.

"Then an artsy guy from Charlottesville talked Tommy into making changes. He had also converted a movie theater in Charlottesville and showed foreign films which was successful because of UVA. He thought Tommy could do the same thing in Fredericksburg and be successful because of Mary Washington College.

"Instead of hosting concerts every other week, it could be open as many days as possible and show classic films and second-run movies. Tommy bought a large screen and 35mm projector.

"I wasn't too crazy about that idea. I wanted to stick to music. I had also met people in the music industry and found that more attractive. I figured I had done what Tommy wanted me to do but with the changes, had no reason to stay anymore. I decided it was time to go back to Nashville as I didn't want to be a movie projector guy."

Steve returned to the Sons of the Beach, WSGI radio and started working with oldies stars.

"Gene Hughes, lead singer for The Casinos, 'Then You Can Tell Me Goodbye' was active in promoting country records throughout the '80s and '90s. He also worked with NARAS – National Association of Recording Arts and Sciences – now called Recording Academy. They host the Grammy Awards and he assisted with many of their events, one being WORST - World's Oldest Rock Stars Together. Gene called me and asked me to be the backup band. This led to other opportunities to work with stars from the '50s, '60s and '70s."

Sons of the Beach in the early 1990's.
Left to right: David Limerick, Buddy Leach, Steve, Marshall
Pearson, Rusty Smith, Jimmy Fulbright, Jimmy Lowry

Alabama Theater

The Alabama Theater opened in 1993 in North Myrtle Beach, South Carolina. A seven-million-dollar project, it features a 2000-seat theater, spectacular backdrops and high energy songs, dancing, and comedy.

"There were three guys that actually owned the Alabama Theater. Not the band like everyone thinks. But the guys gave the band some of the rights so they could use the name."

Vic Schneider and John Haywood were responsible for the entertainment acts at *Opryland Amusement Park*. One day, they called Steve and said, "we want to take you out to lunch."

"We've been hired to put the show together for the Alabama Theater in Myrtle Beach, and we want you to be part of the show," John stated.

"We want you to do 'I've Still Got Sand in my Shoes,' play some oldies, some sax, and do a couple comedy characters like Johnny Cadillac, Duke of Earl and some of the others from the Amusement Park," Vic added.

"It opens in July and we want you on the first show."

Steve beamed at me. "Of course, I accepted! I couldn't refuse the money.

"We rehearsed in Nashville for one month then in Myrtle Beach two weeks before the show. It was a brand-new theater, so we had to work out blocking on the stage and walk through things, getting the show right."

Then John Murray, the stage manager, pulled Steve aside.

"What are you going to do for the pre-show," he asked.

"Pre-show? What's a pre-show?" Steve inquired, his heart racing because he's in shock.

"That's when the comedian comes out fifteen minutes before the show," John replied. "You know comedy, right?"

"Yeah?"

"Well, you're the comedian. What're you going to do?"

Steve was dumbfounded. "I knew I'd signed the contract that mentioned comedy, but I had never done standup comedy in my life!"

Steve had less than two weeks to create the act. He'd done comedy characters with Myron and the Marvells and Our House, so he pulled from those. He even had Johnny Cadillac, but he also wanted to create a new character.

"Gary and Shelva Hudson came to mind. They were friends I had met when they visited the Caymans.

"Gary had been standing in line buying one of our albums and I struck up a conversation with him. You know, like, where are you from?"

"Mt. Airy, North Carolina," Gary answered.

"That's where I grew up! I went on to say I'd attended Beulah Elementary School and long story short, Gary and Shelva lived in Pilot Mountain, North Carolina but owned a second home in Myrtle Beach. We became friends and I would often stay with them whenever I visited in Myrtle Beach.

"When I was trying to name this new character, I decided everyone knew a 'Bubba' and in honor of Gary and Shelva, I named the character 'Bubba Hudson'.

"I dressed like a tacky tourist with baggy white shorts, flowered shirt, brown sandals, black socks and roll up hat. I wore thick glasses, carried a big Myrtle Beach bag on my shoulder and an instamatic camera around my neck. The camera didn't have film in it, but the prop guy put a big flash on it, and it would go off any time I took a picture. That flash attracted everyone's attention.

"A seat was reserved for me on the front row and I would get in the ticket line, talk to the crowd, come inside, start snapping pictures of the posters, everything. Pretty soon, people would start watching me and poking each other. I could hear them snickering and giggling."

When everyone was seated, the lights would dim, the MC would come out and the show would start.

"We have a gentleman in the audience from North Carolina that won a contest. Where are you Mr. Hudson?"

Steve would raise his hand from the front row, then go up on the stage.

"Where are you from, Mr. Hudson?"

"I'm from Pine Ridge, North Carolina," Steve would answer with a deep Southern drawl.

"Tell us about this contest you won," the MC encouraged Steve.

"Well there was a k-roke contest at the Moose Lodge, and I won the trip."

"We're glad you are here and hope you enjoy the show."

Steve turns to go off stage then does an about-face to snap a picture of the MC who has already stepped behind the curtain. Steve looks around, asks someone on the front row "could you take a picture of me so I can put in the newsletter at the Moose Lodge?"

Of course, whoever Steve asks says yes.

Steve goes on the stage, taps on the mic, says "is this thing on?" Starts singing, "Yur Cheatin' Heart."

Steve laughs. "Invariably someone from the audience hollers, 'go Bubba go'.

"This would be the beginning of my fifteen-minute comedy act.

"I was heavier set then and would tell jokes about myself, I didn't want to offend anyone. One was, 'I was in Krogers, standing in line. Behind me was this little boy and his Mama. My beeper went off kinda loud and the little boy started yelling get out the way, Mama, get out the way. The fat man is backing up!'

"Another was, it got so hot the other day, my wife took off all her clothes and stood in front of refrigerator. That was okay with me, but the Sears man didn't seem to like it too much.

"In another, I talked about my three hunting dogs. One was named Einstein because he was so smart; Rambo because he was the meanest; and Mozart because he was the peeingest.

"I did a lot of one-liners, like Bob Hope. All of it was in fun."

Steve would end his first act with, "I'm going to go backstage to say hi to the cast and crew," then step behind the curtain.

"Wow, it's dark back here," the audience can hear Steve's voice.

Suddenly there is a loud crash like the sound of the cymbals from the drummer.

"You must be the drummer," Steve says, and the audience usually laughs.

"What are you doing back here!" another voice shouts.

"And that would lead into the show. After a set, Bubba would come out pushing a broom and the MC would ask what're you doing back here?"

"That man offered me a job," Steve would say.

"You were hired to clean up the show."

"Is that why you have a big dressing room and mine has a mop and bucket?"

"Then he would chase me off the stage," Steve laughs as I shake my head.

The name of the show was *American Pride* and it featured segments for different music styles. Each section had a theme: big band, western, modern country and while the singers and dancers were changing wardrobes between sections, Steve would go out and interact with the MC or the audience.

"I wrote songs and skits for Bubba Hudson that related to each of the sections. For instance, for the western section, I dressed as a cowboy with chaps.

"When I worked on the skit, I was thinking about watching all the old western movies and you'd see these cowboys ride day and night, but they never stopped to go to the bathroom. So, I got the idea to write a song called 'I Gotta Go' to the tune of 'Ghost Riders in the Sky.' Probably the funniest song I did in the whole show.

"*Ever since I was a young boy, I used to enjoy, watching old western movies with Gene Autry and Roy, but there just one thing that I still ponder upon, while at home on the range, there was never a john.*

"*Herding cattle chasing bad guys, eating chili and beans, riding for days with only one pair of jeans, but there's still one thing that I'd like to know what the cowboy would do when he had to go.*

"*Yippie I yay, yippie I yo. Pull over Trigger, I gotta go.*"

"*They'd ride the dusty trail from morning to night, and we'd never see an outhouse in sight, only cacti and tumbleweed, not even a tree for a cowboy to hide behind when he had to go.*

"*Yippie I yay, yippie I yo. Pull over Trigger, I gotta go.*"

"*They'd ride like the wind to the nearest saloon, the only place in town that had a bathroom, they'd fight and brawl and shoot each other dead, the last man standing was first in the head.*"

Steve laughs. "I can't believe I still remember that!"

The second half of the show Steve would be Johnny Cadillac; also impersonate Jake of the Blues Brothers. Then he would be introduced as the recording artist Steve Jarrell and sing "I've Still Got Sand in my Shoes."

"The Opening night was a private showing for dignitaries. We did not do the whole show and Bubba wasn't on that show. But I was in the first act and sang the very first song on the Alabama stage.

"For Opening night, the producer wanted a strong show that introduced the cast as singers and dancers. They decided to start with rock and roll. I sang some of Jerry Lee Lewis' songs at a stage prop piano where the keys moved but no sound. The real piano player was backstage. I did the singing and impersonations of Jerry Lee pounding the piano with my hands and feet.

"My first show as Bubba was in front of 2000 people the next night. And it worked! Bubba became quite popular. Once they got a call from somebody asking about the Bubba Hudson Show. Wanted to know what time it started.

"They always had a different Christmas show and I remember working from two o'clock one afternoon until four the next morning helping to put the first one together.

"During rehearsal, I was dressed like Santa and supposed to sing the Oak Ridge Boys' 'Thank God for Kids.' But I couldn't make it through the song without getting emotional, so they pulled me and had another guy do the scene.

"It was still difficult. In one scene, Johnny Cadillac would come through the fake front door of a house. They built the stage prop in Nashville and had it shipped to Myrtle Beach. By coincidence, the house numbers on the fake door were the same as my house number at home. 401. I was missing my family, and this only added to my misery.

"Johnny Cadillac wore a flashy Christmas coat and it had Christmas lights that would light up. The battery pack was in my pocket and one time it shorted out. That pocket got hot!"

The shows ran for six months – July through the Christmas show. Steve realized during the Christmas show that he had been home three days in six months.

Steve choked up a moment. "Stevie's teacher said he brought an 8x10 picture of me to school, that's how much he missed me."

They wanted Steve to do the next season. Offered more money and he was already one of the highest paid performers on the show.

"But I decided I was going home."

The Alabama Theater celebrated its' 25th Anniversary in 2018. Greg Rowles has been the star of the show for twenty of those years.

"Greg is also from Fredericksburg. I knew his father, Lewis Rowles. If you remember, Lewis was the leader of the band, The Infernos that I played with when I was thirteen. Greg was in Ed McMahon's 'You Can Be A Star' and won as favorite male vocalist. He also worked for *Opryland Amusement Park* before going to work at The Alabama Theater.

"Who would have thought two guys from Fredericksburg would be front men for two popular shows in North Myrtle Beach."

When I interviewed John Hook, he recalled seeing Steve perform at The Alabama Theater when he visited Myrtle Beach.

"I remembered Steve from the 'Carolina Man' interview and by then, Steve had released 'I've Still Got Sand in my Shoes' which had been #1 for several months.

"Steve invited me to come see him at The Alabama Theater where he said he 'sang a couple songs and told jokes.' I quickly realized Steve was bigger than he said. He was introducing all the acts and in between acts, he was telling jokes!

"But when the show was two-thirds over and Steve sang 'I've Still Got Sand in my Shoes' you could have heard a pin drop in that theater. I looked around and the people were transfixed. Nobody moved. They were all focused on Steve. There was something about the story in the song and his mood that nailed it. Steve's delivery and the cast shagging to it made it a beautiful scene.

"I commented to Steve afterwards that most of the people in the audience didn't seem to know the song. He answered 'no, they were country music people, not beach music people.'

"I think Steve's entire career is about having sand in his shoes," John laughed.

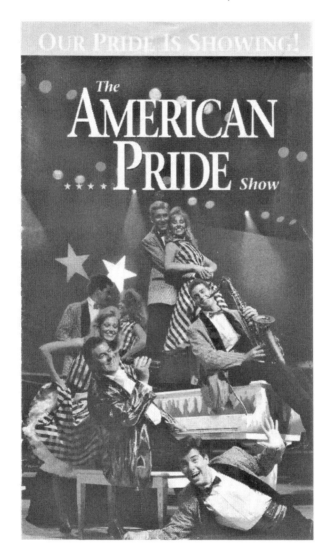

Bubba Hudson

Cowboy Bubba singing "I Gotta Go" Steve's favorite

Steve Jarrell
Winston Salem, NC
Over 30 years of experience, starting with a recording career at 15 with The Prophets in Fredericksburg, VA. In the Beach Music Industry, Steve has recorded such beach hits as "Carolina Man" and the classic "I've Still Got Sand in My Shoes" with his most recent group the "Sons of the Beach". Steve has appeared with groups like the Beach Boys, in "Sweet Dreams" (with Jessica Lange) & many TV specials. ✶

Steve's bio in The Alabama Theater program.

185

Opryland Amusement Park

Steve came home from The Alabama Theater, and returned to *Opryland Amusement Park* where he stayed until they closed three years later.

"The stage was like a barn and on one end was the '50s show and on the other end was a country show. In the center was the green room where everyone relaxed between shows."

There were two country acts. The Tennessee River Boys were there the first year until they left to become Diamond Rio. When they left, Bashful Brother Oswald and Charlie Collins – Oz and Charlie – from Roy Acuff's Smoky Mountain Boys did the show when they weren't performing with Roy Acuff in his Acuff Theater.

"Mr. Acuff was getting up in age and after his wife passed away, he would ride his golf cart along the paved roads between the different venues in the complex. He would come to our set because of Oz and Charlie."

One day, Steve and Roy Acuff happened to be alone in the green room.

"Mr. Acuff, I'm sorry to hear about your wife Mildred dying," I said.

"Thank you, son," Roy Acuff said. "The day Mildred died, I died."

"I remembered thinking, here I am sitting with the King of Country Music having a one on one. Not everybody has the opportunity to share something so personal. He was a great guy."

Ralph Emery had retired from the *Nashville Now* show and Crook and Chase, starring Lorianne Crook and Charlie Chase did their television talk show and country music Top 40 Countdown next door.

"Doc Damon was the announcer for the show and had a guy from Texas that would warm up the audience. He offered instructions, would tell them to clap when he signaled. The guy's mother was ill, and often, I would have to replace him.

"When Vic Schneider and John Haywood came to me, looking for ideas for the '50s side, Karaoke was popular, so I suggested putting a DJ booth in the bed of a red truck. We added a monitor that showed the words and another TV monitor for viewing and invited guests to sing.

"I have to mention Cindy Moore here. She was a girl who impersonated Minnie Pearl in several shows, and she was so good she became the ambassador for the park. She and I would take turns singing, manning the booth, and encouraging people to sing. We sang oldies rock and roll hits doo-wop style.

"For Halloween we decorated the truck and I dressed up as Uncle Fester of the Addams Family. Everyone else dressed as monsters scaring people and every half-hour, we hosted a monster mash and danced with the kids."

During the Christmas holidays, Steve and three other guys sang Country Christmas Carols doo-wop style as the Nutmegs.

"Michael Lusk was Rocco and dressed like a biker, but in real life he sang and played bass with Loretta Lynn, also travelled with Rev. Billy Graham.

"Stacy David was into hot rods and hosted a TV series called *Trucks!* He was Jocco, wore a sport jacket and carried a football.

"Robbie Cheuvront played in the Lonestar Band professionally. He wore a sweater and was the nerd. I was Ace Cariboni and dressed as a mobster.

"We did four twenty-minute shows each night on the stage in front of the truck. It was cold. After each show we would walk over to the *Grand Ole Opry,* which was next door, go in the back door and stand around inside to warm up.

"One night we were singing to the receptionist back there and Bob Whittaker, the general manager of the *Grand Ole Opry* walked by. He stopped and looked at us."

"How would you like to perform on the Grand Ole Opry?'" He asked.

"Sure!" we said. "When?"

"Next," he responded.

Steve laughed out loud.

"You know, everyone says the first time they perform on the stage at the *Grand Ole Opry*, they are scared to death. We didn't have time to be nervous! We were literally the next performance!

"We went on stage, sang 'The Christmas Song' – Chestnuts Roasting on an open fire – then went outside to do our part at the Amusement Park."

189

Opryland Amusement Park brochure featuring Steve on the front cover.

Red Opryland Truck
Cindy Moore, hula hooping with the public. Cindy also dressed
as Minnie Pearl and was the Ambassador for the Park.

Opryland Juke Box Theater for their rock and roll shows.

Steve's favorite of all celebrity pictures - Roy Acuff, The King of Country Music.

The Nutmegs
Left to right: Steve, Stacey David, Robbie Cheuvront, Michael Lusk.

The Nutmegs
Left to right, Stacey David, Robbie Cheuvront, Santa, Steve,
Mrs. Claus, and Michael Lusk.

Rockin' At the Ryman

By July 1998, *Opryland Amusement Park* had been demolished and construction of the *Opry Mall* was underway.

Now that the Park was closed Steve called Vic Schneider, John Haywood, and Bob Whittaker, asked what they were going to do with the Acuff Theater which wasn't being used.

"Don't know," John Haywood replied.

"I'd like to put together an oldie's show," Steve responded. "There are a lot of rock n roll stars that live in and around Nashville. What do you think if I add three girls to perform with the Sons of the Beach, invite some of these stars to do a show and we back them up? Call it the 'Grand Ole Rock N Roll.' Same as *Grand Ole Opry* plays country music? With the Park gone, we need something for the tourists. You could offer two shows for people, country stars one night, rock n roll the next. Sell tickets to both shows at a discount."

A few days later, John Haywood called Steve.

"About your idea, can you get stars to write letters of intent expressing their interest in doing something like this?"

Two weeks later Steve had 32 letters and 13 acts.

"I had people like Pat Upton, Larry Henley, Buddy Knox, Buddy Holly's Crickets, Dobie Gray, Ray Peterson, Clifford Curry, Buzz Cason. I still have those letters."

"Let's think about this," Bob mused.

They called a few days later. "We like the idea, but the *Acuff Theater* is being renovated. What about the *Ryman Auditorium* – the original Grand Ole Opry?"

Steve smiled. "That's what I did. I had thirteen stars and we called it 'Rockin' at the Ryman.' We did a test run on a Saturday night to see if it would work. It was sold out and a huge success.

"I was all ready to put on more shows at the *Acuff* when it was renovated, then I got a call the next week that Ray Stevens wanted to do his show at the *Acuff Theater*. Once again, I was knocked out of an opportunity.

"The thirteen stars had rehearsed; the girls were lined up, we decided, we've got it together, let's do more shows. We'll call it 'Juke Box Gold' and go on tour up and down the East Coast. I averaged eight to ten stars each tour. Each show had a theme and the stars had fifteen minutes to perform.

"We even did one in Central Park in Fredericksburg, Virginia. The first one got rained out, but we had a second night.

"I took care of the booking, production, hotels, payroll, tour buses, you name it. You know, I never had a contract with any of the guys; only got stuck one time when the artist got sick at the last minute. I did several shows but quickly realized it was too much.

"The Artists would get booked elsewhere and it became hard to sell the show. So, I stopped doing it and concentrated on the Sons of the Beach."

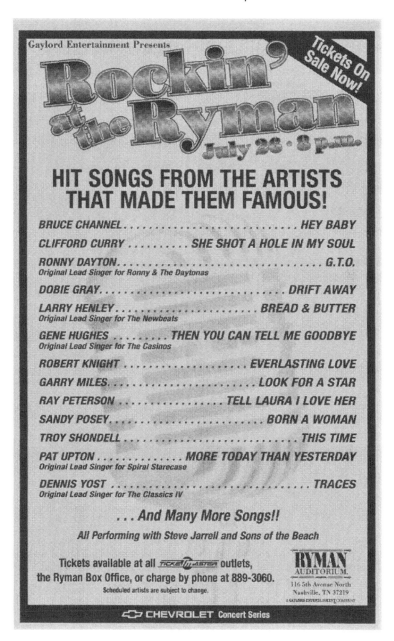

Poster advertising the Rockin' at the Ryman

Proclamation from the Mayor of Nashville in recognition and appreciation of the Rockin' at the Ryman event.

Rock & Roll Graffiti

Larry Black was a popular DJ during the sixties, seventies, and eighties. Today, he is the TV producer of *Country's Family Reunion* and his own *Country Diner* Variety Show.

In 1999, he decided to do a reunion of rock and roll and soul stars from the late '50s and '60s.

It would be called *Rock and Roll Graffiti* and filmed in a TV studio with all the stars sitting in a circle, reminiscing over the old days, their careers travelling on tour buses. Each would individually sing one or two of the songs they were famous for. It was aired on PBS.

Larry had attended the Rockin' at the Ryman Show and asked Steve to be the musical director and the Sons of the Beach backup band.

Steve said he would need to hire three girls to sing background. "I got the three girls that helped with the Juke Box Gold show - Kelli Bruce, Vicky Carrico who sang with Brenda Lee and Etta Britt from Dave and Sugar. They were the cream of crop of the studio women singers."

He and the band rehearsed such songs as: "Dizzy," "Stay," "At The Hop," "Stop In The Name Of Love," "Sugar Shack," "Birds And The Bees," "Everlasting Love," "Rock and Roll Is Here To Stay," "Little GTO," "One, Two, Three," "Little Darlin'," "More Today Than Yesterday" and many others.

The artists included: Jewel Akens, Len Barry, The Browns, John "Bucky" Wilkin (Ronny and the Daytonas), Dave Burgess, Buzz Cason (Garry Miles), Jimmy Clanton, Clifford Curry, Carl

Dobkins, Jr., DJ Fontana (Elvis Presley's drummer), Frankie Ford, Carl Gardner (The Coasters), Jimmy Gilmer (The Fireballs), Gene Hughes (The Casinos), Denny Laine (Moody Blues and Wings), Dickey Lee, Ketty Lester, Jerry Naylor, Gary S. Paxton (Hollywood Argyles), Ray Peterson, Sandy Posey, Jay Proctor (Jay and the Techniques), Jimmie Rodgers, Tommy Roe, Nedra Ross (The Ronettes), Billy Joe Royal, Dee Dee Sharp, Troy Shondell, Dave Somerville (The Diamonds), Joanie Sommers, Dodie Stevens, Joe Terry (Danny and the Juniors), Pat Upton (Spiral Starecase), Otis Williams (The Charms), Maurice Williams (The Zodiacs), Mary Wilson (The Supremes), Dennis Yost (The Classics IV).

"There was so much affection in that show," Steve spoke softly. "No competition, just a need to celebrate the past with friends."

They held a *meet and greet* followed by two days of segments and rehearsals. Steve and the band listened to moving, humbling stories. "They all had stories to tell," Steve said.

Jimmie Rogers, who sang "Honeycomb" talked about being beaten and left on the side of the road to die.

Steve shook his head. "He had to undergo numerous brain surgeries and it was twenty years before he could put a sentence together. There was such a camaraderie, the others on the show helped him sing.

"Ketty Lester talked about how she left singing to be a better Mom to her son."

She had not sung "Love Letters" in thirty years. The first day she took the old sheet music to Steve. She, Spig Davis and Steve rehearsed together.

"I don't know why they want me on the show," she complained meekly. "I'm not really rock and roll."

"Larry Black wants you here," I said.

"She sang the next day and we backed her up. It was so emotional everyone was crying. Everybody had to take a break after she performed!"

Joanie Sommers talked about how she dated Elvis Presley for a time but gave it up when there were always people around.

"I introduced myself to Joanie at the *meet and greet*; didn't tell her I had bought kazoos for the singers to use for her 'Johnny Get Angry' song. After we surprised her with the kazoo solo, she came over, kissed me on the cheek and said 'Steve, I love you.'"

Jimmy Clanton talked about writing "Just a Dream" after being jilted by a girl.

Ray Peterson sang "The Wonder of You" and talked about how Elvis had asked for permission to record it.

Steve chuckled. "Dennis Yost of the Classics IV laughed about playing at a Baptist College and the President of the College made them leave the stage when the students started dancing in the aisles. Dancing wasn't allowed on the campus.

"Jerry Naylor replaced Buddy Holly with the Crickets after the plane crash but admitted nobody could replace Buddy.

"In preparing the show for release Buzz Cason and Gary Paxton were hired to mix the recordings. They called me and asked me to sit in and help them. Said they wanted a younger set of ears. Talk about intimidation! Here I am sitting in a room with two of the most famous producers around.

"We would be listening to a song and they would be telling each other stories. I would hear something that needed to be corrected and would have to interrupt their conversations."

Steve shook his head.

"But I heard some great stories! One was when Buzz Cason and his band the Casuals were backing up Jerry Lee Lewis. They were coming from somewhere and Jerry wanted to see Niagara Falls. So, they drove miles out of their way just to see the Falls. Jerry stepped out of the car, stared at them for a few minutes, got back in the car and said 'let's go home boys. Jerry has seen Niagara Falls.' And then they drove all the way back to Nashville.

"Gary Paxton is a genius when it comes to music production. You might not know the name, but he is the guy that recorded the hit 'Alley Oop' by the Hollywood Argyles.

"First, he got the name from standing on the corner of Hollywood and Argyle streets in California. Back then it was hard to get a record played. You would go to a record store and ask if they had the record and the store would reply 'is it getting air play?' You would go to the radio station and the program director would ask 'is it in stores?' So, it was a catch 22.

"Gary Paxton made his record a hit by going up and down the West coast stopping at the music stores and then telling them he would give them a handful of records if they would keep the copy by the phone. Then he would go to the radio station at that town and they would ask the question 'is in stores?' They would call and the owner who would say, 'yeah, it's right here by the phone.'

"That's how Ally Oop became a hit!

"Another great story from Gary was he was living in Los Angeles and bought an old mixing console from a movie studio. He rented an old house, put the console in the living room of the house, knocked a hole in the floor going to the basement and would hang all the mics down the hole into the basement.

"He produced and engineered some of those great recordings by the Association that way. They would come to the basement and record their parts. It was so hot in the basement they would stand in their bathing suits and play.

"Back to the Rock & Roll Graffiti production," Steve brought me back to our interview, "that PBS collection is rare, and nothing has been done since! I made a lot of friends those two days and still stay in touch with a lot of them.

"Many of their bands have disbanded and the Sons of the Beach are often asked to back the leaders of the bands at performances. When we played with Dennis Yost, we backed him up as the Classics IV.

"Bucky Wilkin was also a member of Ronny and Daytonas and we sometimes backed him up as the Daytonas.

"The door kept opening after that project. Denny Laine led to Mr. Sid. Remind me to tell you about that.

"In 2014, Mary Wilson with The Supremes invited me to the RoosterTail in Detroit for Levi Stubs' 50th Anniversary of the Four Tops. The RoosterTail is where Motown artists like Aretha Franklin, Temptations, Four Tops jam together. Once again, I took Jimmy Franklin, Charles Weimer and Bootsie Howard with me.

"You know, you go to a party and sometimes there will be a small band off to the side performing while everyone socializes? Not there. Those 'small bands' were Motown artists! I was ten feet away from The Temptations and in awe. It was like a concert to me.

"Aretha came in with a big thing of flowers, her bodyguard rushed her off the stage after she sang. Everybody was used to being there, but I sat in the window with my mouth open. I was singing along with The Tops and Levi Stubb's younger sister asked, 'Where did a white boy like you learn to sing like that?'

"I have a picture of Charles Weimer and me with The Temptations. Then we learned that Ian Gillan and Deep Purple were in town so after our party with the Motown stars, we took a cab over to the hotel and partied with Deep Purple till four in the morning. Then we got on a plane at six in the morning to come home. I did a radio show a couple hours later.

By being in the right place at the right time I was able meet a lot of rock and roll stars, but I was always working my butt off. I still stay in touch with a lot of the stars today and call Ketty Lester every year on her birthday.

Left to right: Camera man, Kelly Bruce, Vicki Carrico, Etta Britt, Randy Layne, Milton Cavender, Steve, Larry Black, Producer.

Dave Somerville (The Diamonds), Joanie Sommers and Steve after rehearsal.

Denny Laine (Moody Blues. Paul McCartney and Wings), Jimmie Rodgers and Steve.

Left to Right: Carl Gardner (The Coasters), Mary Wilson (The Supremes), Steve and Dodie Stevens.

Steve, Charles Weimer and The Temptations
At the RoosterTail in Detroit for Levi Stubs' 50th Anniversary
of the Four Tops in 2014.

All the stars and Band on the Rock & Roll Graffiti Show taping.

"Mr. Sid"

Denny Laine was a founding member of the Moody Blues and inducted into the Rock and Roll Hall of Fame in 2018. He also played with Paul McCartney and Wings, 1971-1981.

Denny and Steve remained friends after the *Rock & Roll Graffiti* tribute.

"In July 2005, Denny was performing at a benefit for Mike Smith of the Dave Clark Five in New York and he sent me tickets to the show.

"Mike had fallen off a fence and broken his neck, and Paul Shaffer from the David Letterman Show organized the event at B.B. King's Blues Club in New York City.

"It was a HUGE show – The Zombies, Peter and Gordon, Billy J. Kramer, The Fab Faux and Denny performed. I think Max Weinberg and his group from the Conan O'Brien show were also part of the show. The place was packed.

"I sat beside an older gentleman on the front row and people kept coming up to shake his hand. I thought to myself, this guy was somebody."

Then Steve heard someone refer the gentleman as Mr. Bernstein.

"Are you Sid Bernstein, the man who started the Beatles invasion?" I inquired.

"Why yes, I am," he answered in a soft voice.

Steve laughed. "I'm glad. The way everyone has been greeting you, I was worried I might be sitting beside the Godfather."

When Sid Bernstein learned Steve was from Nashville, he started calling him 'Tennessee.' Steve called him 'Mr. Sid.'

"I bet you've never seen anything like this," Mr. Sid commented.

"Shucks, this ain't nothing. We've got the *Grand Ole Opry* where I live."

After the show, Mr. Sid said, "Stay in touch, with me, Tennessee. I like you."

Days later, Steve called Mr. Sid, offered to give him a tour of the *Grand Ole Opry* whenever he was down South.

"I might take you up on that," Mr. Sid said. "I've never been there. Do you know Steve Wariner?"

"No," I replied, "but my friend Buzz Cason does."

"I'd like to get in touch with Steve. He's been overlooked and I'd like to present him at Carnegie Hall."

Steve knew that Mr. Sid had written two books – *It's Sid Bernstein Calling* and *Not Just the Beatles.*

"What I'd really like to do is come down and do a book signing and lecture," Mr. Sid continued.

"I don't know anything about that but let me see what I can do," I answered. Then I called the Mike Curb School of Music to see if they had a Lecture Series. Asked if they would like to have Sid Bernstein speak.

"I gave them his number but asked if they could do it on a Wednesday so I could take Mr. Sid to the *Grand Ole Opry* on Tuesday night.

"Then I called a friend who was a substitute drummer at the Opry. Remember, if you knew a member of the band you could get backstage. He hooked me up and when Mr. Sid came with his attorney, I took him to the *Opry*. We sat backstage on one of the church pews, and he got to meet Little Jimmy Dickins and others that appeared that night. I have some pictures somewhere around here.

"On Wednesday, Mr. Sid did the lecture and book signing, which had a huge turnout. The President of the college took us out to dinner which was nice." Steve chuckled. "Afterwards, Mr. Sid, who was 89 or 90 at this time, said he was tired but wouldn't mind some ice cream, so I took him to get some ice cream before he turned in.

"The next day Mr. Sid had lunch with Steve Wariner who took him to the airport."

Mr. Sid knew Steve had a radio show and had given Steve a Neville Skelly CD he was currently producing in Liverpool.

"I played the CD on my show the next day and Mr. Sid heard it on the radio when they were on the way to the airport. He called to say I was the first DJ in America to play Neville Skelly."

Months later, Steve and the Sons of the Beach did a benefit with a lot of other country stars for the *Robertson County Reads* program. It was a fundraiser for Dolly Parton's state-wide project to give books to youngsters in the state. The President of the Rock and Roll Hall of Fame in Cleveland attended the show and met Steve.

The next time Steve talked with Mr. Sid he asked if he would like to do a lecture and book signing at the Rock and Roll Hall of Fame.

"I certainly would," he replied.

Once again, Steve said, "I don't know anything about that but let me see what I can do. Having met the President recently, I gave him a call and asked him if he would like to have Mr. Sid do a lecture and book signing there. He said of course and we arranged it for Mr. Sid. That book signing was also very successful.

"Holly Powers booked us on a show for CheapCaribbean.com who was putting on a large Caribbean Convention in Meadowland, New Jersey, and Mr. Sid came to that. As a matter of fact, I wrote the theme song for CheapCaribbean.com and we performed it there on the show."

A few months later, Mr. Sid invited Steve to the 40th Anniversary of the Beatles show he was doing in New York City.

"I'm bringing Neville Skelly from Liverpool to perform and to let everyone know I am still promoting guys forty years after the Beatles. I want you to come and introduce Neville."

Steve laughed. "I said I would walk if I had too.

"Mr. Sid introduced me to Deidre Broderick, a songwriter who was working on a documentary film about him. She was also on the show as was Kate Taylor, James Taylor's sister.

"I hadn't planned to do more than introduce Neville Skelly, but I ended up filling in for a band that was unable to get there.

"That year was the second worst snowstorm in New York City history. Mr. Sid had hired a Beatles Tribute band from New Jersey, and they were snowed in. The weather didn't stop the people from attending though. The show was sold out and the people travelled the subway.

"Mr. Sid was upset, didn't know what to do about that twenty-minute slot. I told him I knew the songs and had done some stand-up comedy. I could do a little comedy show and sing some songs."

"You saved my show! You saved my show!" Mr. Sid said over and over at the end of the show.

"I just shrugged my shoulders. Said I happened to be here."

In 2011, Steve received a call from Mr. Sid who was 92 at the time.

"I've worked with all these people; I want to make a CD. Deidre is producing it. Will you come to play the sax and sing background?"

"I felt so honored," Steve exclaimed. "I travelled to New York and we spent part of a day in St. Stephens Cathedral with four mics, two on my sax and two in rear of the church to get the ambiance."

Steve smiled. "Made me sound so good."

The name of the CD was "Sid Bernstein Presents." He sang songs by Tony Bennett, John Lennon, Roy Orbison and others he knew or promoted. Steve also sang background and played "I Left My Heart in San Francisco" on his sax.

"The album cover has two pictures of us, sitting at Second Avenue Deli in New York. It was released on Valentine's Day, 2012."

A year later, August 21, 2013, Steve got a phone call that Mr. Sid had died.

"I loved Mr. Sid like you would a grandfather. I didn't know my own grandfathers. My Dad's father died when I was five or six and I hardly knew my mother's father at all. So, Mr. Sid has a special place in my heart. He accomplished so much and was an amazing man. I miss him. You don't often meet guys like that in the music business."

Mr. Sid at Elliston Place Ice Cream Parlor in Nashville enjoying ice cream

Steve with Mr. Sid at the Second Avenue Deli in New York.

Steve and the legendary DJ Joey Reynolds at the Sid Bernstein Show.

Deidre Broderick, songwriter, looking at Steve during his comedy skit.

Deidre Broderick and Mr. Sid working on the album.

Cancun, Mexico

In the 1990's, the Sons of the Beach also performed at the Royal Resort in Cancun, Mexico. "I had met Holly Powers, a tourism and event planning expert who had connections there. She booked us on several different occasions.

"Marshall and I went down a week before the show to rent the sound equipment and do the preliminary setup. The Royal Resort stage is one of the most elaborate stages we've ever performed on.

"The husband of one of the ladies that worked at the resort owned a Mexican restaurant. One night we set up outside his restaurant and put on a show. He loved it! Hired a mariachi band to join us outside."

*The Royal Resort, Cancun, Mexico.
One of their most elaborate venues.*

Still Rockin'

The Sons of the Beach played at the 2000 Republican National Convention in Pennsylvania and George Bush's Victory Party on election night.

"This was the time they had *chad* problems with the votes in Florida. On election night, we were set up at the Mayflower Hotel in Washington, D.C. and across from us were cameras from all over the world.

"Everybody was sitting around, waiting, watching the screens for the Florida results. Then one by one, people, and cameras, started leaving. There was a guy there with a walkie talkie and he would tell us to do two more songs. Then finally he said 'you might as well go upstairs and go to bed. They're not going to pick the President tonight.'

"We had lost all that publicity because of the chad problems. I wrote a song, 'My Little Chad.' The guys and I recorded it and some of the talk shows played it. Occasionally, they will replay it."

"The Sons of the Beach has been a steppingstone for some of the guys. A drummer went on to play with Tim McGraw; a trumpet player left to be in Delbert McClinton's band. A sax player went with George Thorogood and the Destroyers.

"I have been with the current guys for thirty years now and there has never been a dull moment."

Steve and the Sons of the Beach were invited to perform with The Tams at the Corvette Museum in Bowling Green, Kentucky.

"Then they realized they already had a beach group with The Tams. I didn't want to lose the gig, so I took one of my Johnny Cadillac pictures, went on the website and created a new promo for 'Johnny Vette and the Stingrays,' keeping in tune with the Corvette Museum. They thought that was cool!

I told Steve that Randy Layne, Spig Davis and Marshall Pearson all three mentioned this event to which Steve laughed out loud.

"I had this gold sequined jacket I planned to wear and painted some cowboy boots gold to match it. During the performance, my feet and ankles swelled up and I couldn't get the boots off! The Tams and the guys in the band had a hardest time pulling those boots off!

"Another time, we stayed at a motel after a gig. I had hired a soundman who carried all the small equipment in his trailer. The keyboard player used my keys to get his stuff from the trailer, then put the keys in his pocket. After the performance, the keyboard player left to go home. With my keys in his pockets!

"I was worrying about how to get home and the soundman said he could get my truck started. How are you going to do that?" I asked.

"I used to steal cars in my younger days."

"Then he hotwired my truck!

"We also had a keyboard player that would talk to his dog and he didn't even have a dog! Maybe it was that same keyboard player," Steve laughed.

Randy Layne played guitar and recalled when he first started working with the group.

"I was the new guy at the time and we were on the way to a gig in Memphis. We travelled in two vehicles and I rode with Steve in the second car with all the equipment. We had car trouble and the guys in front of us were too far ahead to notice. This was before cell phones. Steve had to rent a U-Haul truck and I'm the new guy helping him transfer all of the equipment. We were ninety minutes late but still got there in time for the performance. He was paying the guys at the end of the show and didn't have too much money left for himself after paying for the U-Haul truck. I remember saying I guess that's the price you pay for being the leader.

"At one time, Steve was heavier, and we were all getting dressed for a show. Steve was wearing these white pants and Hawaiian shirt and I said, 'be careful you might pop a button. Put somebody's eye out. I couldn't have timed it better because suddenly a button popped off and flew across the room. We all laughed. 'Anyone hurt?' I hollered.

"Steve was always joking, 'guess who I talked to today.' We would say off the wall names. Paul McCartney? Queen Elizabeth? Sure enough, it would be someone famous.

"I've been with Steve for thirty years," Randy ended our phone conversation. "He's a fine, fine fellow. Honest to a fault."

Randy is retired but still does recording sessions and sings in his church. COVID has restricted their performances for now but they hope to get back on the circuit soon.

David "Spig" Davis played keyboard and met Steve when they performed together in the Winters Brothers Band at a Charlie Daniels event in the late '70s. When the Sons of the Beach were reorganizing in the early 1990's, Spig auditioned for the piano player and has been with him since.

He recalled a Fourth of July event. "We were going to sing 'God Bless America' and the band got started in the wrong key." Spig chuckled. "It wasn't in Steve's range, but he plowed through it anyway.

"Steve has a way of winning the audiences," Spig added. "People would be expecting a country group and he had a charisma that would win them over."

Marshall agreed. "Wherever we had a gig, Steve would get the crowd involved. He did his research ahead of time. Got to know the town and people so he could relate to the audience."

Spig is an associate pastor in a church and still plays, writes songs. He has also helped Steve put some of his songs to music.

Marshall played the drums and sang. He also worked a nine-to-five job in construction and is still in the construction business. "I'm in the corporate office, not in the field where I'd much rather be."

Marshall also plays with a blues band as well as with Steve whenever he needs him.

All three men were very complimentary of Steve. Randy and Spig both said he is honest to a fault; Marshall stated Steve is a class act, straight up kind of guy.

I sensed a brotherly bond. They have become family, share events and music travels. They may not talk to each other weekly but are there for each other if need be.

As recording artists retired from the music business, their touring bands also disbanded. Whenever the artist would be invited to perform, they would ask the Sons of the Beach to be their backup band and be recognized as the artist's original band.

When General Motors reintroduced the GTO, Ronny and the Daytonas were invited for a performance at the Woodward Dream Cruise, a huge classic car event held outside Detroit along Woodward Avenue. Bucky Wilkin (aka Ronny), writer and singer of "Little GTO" asked Steve and the Sons of the Beach to back him and Buzz Cason as the Daytonas.

Ronny and the Daytonas aka Sons of the Beach
Left to right: Randy Layne, Buzz Cason, Jim Liner, Bucky Wilkin (Ronny
Dayton), Steve, Ted Hillary and Marshall Pearson.

The Sons of the Beach in the 1990's.
Left to right: Randy Layne, Milton Cavender, Steve, Marshall Pearson,
Chuck Schumacher, Dave "Spig" Davis.

The Sons of the Beach in 2020.
Randy Layne, Marshall Pearson, Steve, Dave "Spig" Davis and
Rick Maness.

DaddyO on the PatiO

When Steve and Cindy bought the house in Ashland City in 1983, he began to dabble in radio broadcasting as another means of supporting his family.

"There was a brand-new station, WAJN where radio veteran Joe Roberts gave me a job and taught me all I know about broadcasting."

He only stayed there a few months before dropping out to work at *Opryland Amusement Park*.

"When we moved to Springfield after the Caymans, I got a call from WDBL AM/FM. They wanted to broadcast live at a *Relay for Life* event. It was also the station's 50th anniversary so they planned to set up a booth at the event and play '50s music. Only problem, '50s music was a different format for the station, and they didn't have many of the records."

"Steve Jarrell's back in town," one of the DJ's suggested, "he has a wealth of records."

"They called, asked if I would share my collection. I said sure and offered to DJ the event."

The following week, people began calling the station because they liked his show.

Steve smiled. "The station contacted me, said they wanted to hire me but couldn't afford me!

"I was making money off the band, so I offered to sell ads on the show and split the proceeds fifty-fifty with the station. Then the corporate company offered to put me on the payroll. I said I was happy with the deal we had."

"We can keep the deal and pay you too," they responded. "We don't want to lose you! This is the first time the station has made the Arbitron Ratings in Nashville radio."

Steve chuckled. "Then they sold the station! But Neil and Jo Petersen with WSGI offered me a job where I stayed for fifteen years. They were wonderful people to work for and are great friends. Would let me off whenever I needed to be off. I was sad to leave them."

Steve worked ten in the morning to two in the afternoon. He often took thirty to fifty song requests each day and was considered by many to be a walking encyclopedia of the music business. Phones would ring off the wall.

Life settled down a little. He still played with Sons of the Beach but had more flexibility to work. Cindy was Director of the Robertson County Senior Citizen Center.

"There were lots of factories in the town. Wilson Sporting Goods, Holly Carburetors, Frigidaire, several more. I played oldies, rhythm and blues and everyone listened while they worked. I called the show *Daddy-O on the Patio* and made an impression.

"I had listened to radio as a child. Remember, Oscar *Daddy Oh* Alexander on WAAA. When I decided to go into radio, *Daddy Oh* had passed away but I wanted to keep his legacy alive because he meant so much to me as a youngster.

"I called WAAA and talked to Mutter D. Evans, the owner of the station. She was the first black owner in North Carolina. I told her my story and said I wanted to keep *Daddy Oh's* legacy alive. Asked if I could get permission from his family to do so. She said she would check. She called me back. Said she spoke with his daughter who responded, 'if he can walk the walk and talk the talk.'

"My reply was as James Brown once said, 'Don't worry about the peeling falling from the ceiling, just be in motion when you get the notion.' She called back a couple days later to say I had the family's blessing to use the name.

"I played oldies, soul music, rock and roll and Carolina Beach music and had lots of listeners."

People would call from the warehouses and in one instance, Steve learned of a woman that was fired because she apparently listened to the radio too much.

"When they said she couldn't have her radio at work, she defied them and was fired."

Another time, a woman called and asked, "Daddy-Oh, can I ask you a question? What side of the bread do you put the butter on?"

"What?" I asked, totally confused.

"I mean, are you black or white?"

"I'm whatever color you want me to be," I laughed.

"When I retired from the radio, a lady who had lost her husband telephoned to say she would miss me."

"My husband used to be my 'number one,'" she said, "Now you are."

"Local businesses would recognize me for my work and invited me to emcee events. One business, *Wilson's Sporting Goods*, made a miniature golf bag with 'DaddyO on the PatiO' on it.

"*Maddy's Hot Dogs* created the 'Daddy-O-Dog' because I would go there a lot and get a hot dog with chili, onions, mustard and coleslaw on it."

Steve started a *Music in the Park* with the Director of Parks and Recreation, Leslie Dean. The Mayor gave him the key to the city, and he was voted best radio DJ in Robertson County.

Steve closed his last show with a salute to the military, emergency responders, law enforcement and school bus drivers by playing Ray Charles' 'America the Beautiful' and received a letter of appreciation from the Tennessee State Senator Kerry Roberts thanking him for ending with the tribute.

Kay Brooks

"In a lot of ways, I miss the people. You know, there's playing records, and then there's playing records that mean something to people."

In 2013, when Steve moved to Fredericksburg after his divorce, he contacted Keith Angstadt, a long-time friend and radio man in the city. Keith also owned an internet radio station, *mybnr.com* (Baltimore Network Radio) and he made a spot for Steve to do his show. Being back in Fredericksburg, his friends would often stop by to visit.

"I loved doing the internet show because I had listeners from all over the world. One of the listeners was Terri Barker. Turns out, Terri knew me from her college days, although I didn't know her. She also worked part time as bookkeeper for Jarrell Industries, and would sign my checks when I worked there for my Uncle Oran Jarrell!

"In 2013, Terri was working for Centennial Broadcasting, the company that owns WFVA in Fredericksburg. She tried to get the manager of WFVA to hire me for the station. Still, I didn't know who she was.

"Whenever I would make a mistake on *mybnr.com*, she would call me with the answers. She knows more about oldies than I do!"

Terri talked Steve into doing a CD of the fifty years of his songs for friends and family. When Steve left the radio, she took the role as his PR person.

"I hate to promote myself. It's hard for me to honk my own horn other than a sax."

Steve's live radio studio in the basement of his home.

Steve doing his "DaddyO on the PatiO" radio show.

Steve with Ronny McDowell and Billy Joe Royal, frequent visitors on his "DaddyO on the PatiO" show.

Plaque recognizing the Daddy-O-Dog at Maddy's Hot Dogs.

Letter from Senator Kerry Roberts.

Recognition & Awards

In September 2001, Steve received a call from a reporter stating he had been nominated for the South Carolina Rhythm and Blues Music Hall of Fame.

"What? Me? Are you sure there hasn't been some mistake?"

Clifford Curry had nominated Steve and Skipper Hough, a spokesman for the Hall of Fame agreed. Stated Steve had "been such a part of beach music, both as a performer and as someone who has helped to spread the music in so many different ways."

The Hall of Fame's Board of Directors – performers, club owners, recording industry folk – unanimously approved it, making Steve the first white performer to be inducted into the Hall of Fame.

Steve was the first white performer to be inducted into the South Carolina Rhythm and Blues Music Hall of Fame.

"Whatever the Hall's reason, I was just so proud to be part of this group of fabulous performers."

On October 26-28, 2001, Steve, Jackie Wilson, The Coasters, Smokey Robinson and thirteen others were conscripted into the Hall of Fame of beach music. Each performed before their peers that weekend.

The Carolina Beach Music Hall of Fame honors the hard work, promotion, preservation, and ongoing influence of performers, songwriters, radio personalities and DJ's and others involved in beach music.

It began in 1995 in Salisbury, North Carolina, but in 1998, was moved to North Myrtle Beach, South Carolina where it became a festive celebration of music the second weekend in November of each year. Entertainers perform at various clubs and venues on Friday and Saturday nights followed by the awards show on Sunday afternoon.

Inductees are nominated by their peers and voted on by the Executive Board and Board of Directors of the Carolina Beach Music professionals.

In 2005, Clarence Carter, Willie Tee, Otis Pope, Jr. Jimmy Cavallo and Steve were inducted into the Carolina Beach Music Hall of Fame.

In 2005, Steve was inducted into the Carolina Beach Music Hall of Fame.

Another award he won in 2005 was the Billy Scott Lifetime Achievement Award from the Beach Music Association International. Billy Scott was considered by many as an ambassador of beach music. He died in 2012.

A few years ago, an Anchor Beach Music Station – The Surf Myrtle Beach – ran a contest for listeners to vote on the Top 20 All Time beach music songs and "I've Still Got Sand in my Shoes" was #8.

Certificate of Recognition from the
South Carolina Rhythm and Blues Hall of Fame.

Jeff Cook of The Alabama Band, presenting Steve with the Beach Music Hall of Fame Award, 2005

Steve, Willie Tee and Clarence Carter after being inducted into the Carolina Beach Music Hall of Fame, 2005.

*Clifford Curry, Otis "Big Daddy" Williams of The Charms
and Steve at Beach Music Day, Raleigh, N.C. May 25, 2005*

Sons of Beach Duos

"Remember PB? Paul Bruening? The friend that heard me singing in Hawaii and invited me to move in with him?

"He wasn't a musician, but when Gene Wells and I played with the Rotations, PB would hang around.

"PB and Gene were both pharmacists and they owned a cottage in Hope Town Bahamas. It was just a little island with a lighthouse, a few restaurants and two or three small resorts on it. You would fly down to Marsh Harbor then take a twenty-minute boat ride to the island.

"After I organized the *Last Chance Dance* in Fredericksburg – remind me to tell you about that – they called me, wanted me to come to Hope Town, put together some live entertainment.

"Gene still had his keyboard and knew a lot of the locals there.

"Hope Town had never had live entertainment on the island and Gene and PB wanted to put a group together that could do jam sessions for entertainment.

"They flew me down there, and I went around to the restaurants and bars, talked to the staff. Asked if they knew any locals that played music.

"I found a guitar player who was from Nashville. He asked if I knew the Wooten Brothers. I figured if he jammed with the Wooten Brothers, he knew music.

"I found another guy that owned a brick-laying and concrete company that could also play the guitar.

"I went to Marsh Harbor, a nearby island and found a bass player.

"Then we needed a drummer. Gene knew one – a big Bohemian guy named Junior Bernard who worked at the *Sea Spray Marina.* He said he'd love to play with us, only problem, he didn't have any drums. So, Gene and PB took the boat to Marsh Harbor, found a set for $800 in this Floor Covering/Music Store." Steve chuckled. "That's how diversified the businesses are down there.

"Within a week we had a band. Sang a mixture of American songs and their native songs. The whole idea was to have a jam session that weekend at the house and invite some of the people from the island for a small show.

"Well, everyone came to hear us.

"It was so successful PB, Gene and I went back a year later for a 'beginning of season party' and the whole island came! They closed the businesses, and everybody brought food. We ended up having to move out into the yard."

Because Gene and PB had the cottage there, they joined in many of the community events, even sponsored a softball team.

After that first show, the locals stayed together and renamed themselves the Hope Town Islanders, became the house band at the *Sea Spray Marina.*

Gene never pursued music because of being a pharmacist but Steve always felt Gene missed the excitement.

"Gene also owned the *Blue Marlin Motel* and whenever we played in Virginia Beach we stayed at the *Blue Marlin.* We would sit around, talk about the road life and I would sometimes catch a look of envy on Gene's face. So, he and I decided to team up as a duo and I called us Sons of the Beach II."

Dan Sullivan owned the *Abaco Inn* on Abaco Island in the Bahamas. He was also from Nashville and knew about the

Sons of the Beach. When Steve and Gene started working together as a duo Dan would have them perform at the Inn three days at a time. They were occasionally joined by a good friend, Doug Bell from Bellevue Cadillac, a Neo-swing group from New England.

"We would do the first night for the locals with the Hope Town Islanders; the second night and third afternoon we sang at the *Abaco Inn*. I looked at it as a free trip to the Bahamas, where I got paid to sing."

Because it was just the two of them, Steve and Gene began using music tracks for backup.

"I never thought much of the music tracks, I preferred live entertainment but didn't mind going to the Bahamas and getting paid to use the tracks.

"Then we started getting calls for everywhere, Florida, Georgia, as far north as New York City. Even Fairview Beach. I couldn't afford to take the entire band to Virginia so Gene Wells and I would perform there as Sons of Beach II with the music tracks.

"I continued to do Sons of Beach here in Nashville, then once a month flew to Virginia to work in Fairview Beach, Colonial Beach or Tappahannock."

Steve promoted both bands on his website.

"Lee Quisenberry was a multi-talented musician. His father was Don Quisenberry who played with Bill Deal and the Rhondels and was a good friend to Gene and me.

"Lee was running Fat Ammons Band and trying to raise a family. So, Gene made Lee night clerk at the *Blue Marlin* where he worked midnight to eight in the morning. If Lee needed to get off for his band, Gene would let him off.

"The motel had a small lobby, reservation desk, one-way glass window and door that was locked at night. Anyone that came in after hours would buzz Lee from the back room.

"Lee had his equipment set up in that office behind the desk and would stay back there making the music tracks for us to work with at the Bahamas.

"Then Gene developed a brain tumor. We thought he would pull through so Lee substituted for Gene in the duo. He knew all the songs because he had recorded them. Sadly, Gene died, and Lee came in with me full-time on the road as the duo. He plays keyboards, trumpet and provides lead vocals. Sometimes we almost sound like an entire band!"

Steve also formed a Sons of the Beach Duo with Michael Sheets during his brief stay in North Myrtle Beach where they performed at various venues.

Steve first met Ken Posey when he moved to Nashville and joined Myron and the Marvells. Steve moved on but Ken was with the Marvells for ten years.

When Steve returned to Nashville in 2017, he happened to see Ken performing with Jimmy Church, a well-known Nashville performer.

"Ken is incredibly talented; a lot like Lee Quisenberry in the ability to play great keyboards, trumpets, and sing. With Ken's prior experience, with the Marvells, he knew a lot of the oldie's songs. I knew we would be a perfect fit as a Duo in Nashville.

"It has worked out well because Ken and his son have their own full band together and I still have the Sons of the Beach, so the two of us together are able to work the smaller venues that can't afford the full bands."

Paul "PB" Bruening and Gene Wells at Hope Town.

Steve and Gene Wells standing outside PB's Place.

Hope Island Sons of the Beach Tour Bus.

Doug Bell from Bellevue Cadillac, Steve Jarrell and Gene Wells performing at the Abaco Inn in the Bahamas.

Gene Wells

Gene Wells and Steve as Sons of Beach II at Abaco Inn, Hope Town, Bahamas.

Steve and Gene Wells painted on the floor of the original Starlight Pavilion, now called Tim's II in Fairview Beach. Steve first performed there in 1963 with Don and the X-Citers, then the Prophets. Gene started there in 1967 with The Rotations. Both performed there in later years as Sons of Beach II.

Steve and Lee Quisenberry, Sons of Beach II in Virginia.

Michael Sheets, Sons of Beach II in North Myrtle Beach.

Steve and Ken Posey, Sons of Beach II in Nashville.

Sons of Beach Fredericksburg
Steve's backup whenever he performs in Fredericksburg.
Left to right, Don Ballard, John Wayne Edwards, Tom
Waite, Jim Ring, Hal Revercomb, Carey Leitch, and Lee
Quisenberry.

Family

Steve loves his family but missed out on many events.

"I wasn't always at home; but they were supportive of all I did. Music and being a member of the Sons of the Beach was our job. It's how we supported our families.

"The wives and kids didn't come to all of our shows because they had their own careers and busy lives. It's not like high school where the girls we dated came to the dances.

"With my busy schedule and Cindy's involvement in the community, we drifted apart after 33 years of marriage.

"But we are still friends."

His children have always been the most important part of Steve's life and he would invite them up on the stage if they were at a performance.

Cindy and Steve during their dating days.

Steve and Cindy dressed for one of the benefits.

Austin Leigh Jarrell and Dottie West at Cayman Islands.

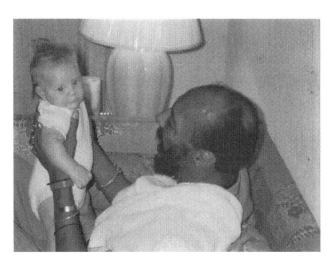

Richie Havens holding Stephen Franklin Jarrell, Jr. at Cayman Islands.

Austin, age three, snorkeling in the pool at Treasure Island Resort, Cayman Islands, 1987

Austin and Stephen with his hands over his ears because Austin would always tell him what to do. She still does!

Stephen and Austin singing "Hey Baby" on stage with Dad.

Stephen studied sax in school. This is the first time he played with Steve at the old Fredericksburg Elk Lodge for a New Year's Eve party in 1999.

Austin Leigh Jarrell

Stephen Franklin Jarrell, Jr.

Giving Back

Steve and the Sons of the Beach often perform free of charge for special causes. Steve also participates individually. Being in the radio, he became part of the community, was aware of special needs and often initiated the fundraisers.

Grateful for his successes, he has supported musician friends that have faced medical issues and mounting hospital bills.

"The early years of rock and roll was a rough life. We didn't have tour buses or fly from gig to gig; we drove cars, travelled in caravans across the country. Rehearsed for long hours after gigs.

"Being in the circuit with the oldies stars, we keep in touch, look out for each other, do benefits whenever a medical crisis might hit. Oftentimes it will be a last-minute call looking for backup or to play the sax at a fundraiser. There is often no time for rehearsal.

"Sometimes I'll get the call and never know the person the benefit is for."

When Dennis Yost of The Classic IV fell and suffered a brain injury in 2006, Steve joined with fellow artists Jon "Bowzer" Bauman (Sha Na Na), Mark Volman (The Turtles), Chuck Negron (Three Dog Night), Clifford Curry, Pat Upton (Spiral Starecase), Denny Laine (Moody Blues & Wings) and many others to do a benefit for him at *Rhino's Live* in Cincinnati, Ohio on March 25, 2007.

Kay Brooks
~ Kaia Jergenson ~

In 2000, Kaia Jergenson was an eighteen-year-old standout basketball player at Lipscomb University, a small religious college in Tennessee.

"Kaia wanted to be a doctor but contracted meningococcal meningitis her freshman year. Staff and students in the school coordinated a round-the-clock prayer vigil to the point that someone prayed for Kaia every minute she lay unconscious in the hospital."

The prayers saved Kaia's life but both legs had to be amputated below the knee as well as three fingers from her writing hand.

College students organized bake sales, dormitory donation drives, "milk jugs of change" to defray some of the $130,000 medical expenses.

"I read about her losing her legs in the newspaper. We had finished a gig and were taking the equipment down, and I suggested putting something together to raise some money for her family. The guys were okay with it, so I called around and other musicians either said, 'yeah, book me' or offered a donation. We had it at the college for free, the sound was free, everything was free. Had old-timey posters donated by a local business. We even autographed the posters and sold them. All the money went to Kaia.

"The show was opened by Michael McDonald and Ray Peterson. What was especially fun for me was singing 'Soul Man' with Steve Cropper who played guitar with Sam and Dave who recorded it and the Blues Brothers who sang it in their movie. You know, 'Steve' is mentioned in the song and we would get to the part of the song where they would say 'Play it Steve!' and there Steve was! The real deal!

"After the show, a TV reporter interviewed me and asked why we did the show. I simply said a bunch of friends wanted to do it and 100% of the profits went to Kaia's medical expenses. Turns out the reporter was doing one of those investigative news segments about how fundraising organizations never had much money left over to give to the people they were doing the fundraiser for."

The next night, the journalist reported, "Here comes Steve Jarrell, a guy who is not in the fundraising business, but every dime went to Kaia."

~ Ray Peterson ~

"Ray Peterson was an amazing man. He sang 'Tell Laura I Love Her', 'Corinna, Corrina' and 'The Wonder of You.'

"He had polio in both legs early in life and was encouraged to sing to help his breathing, play golf because of his legs. He always had to be in motion.

"He had cancer and didn't tell anyone about it for the longest time. We held a benefit for him in Springfield on Saturday, May 31, 2005. It was so well attended; we had a tour bus come from Cincinnati, Ohio to Springfield, Tennessee. There were fifteen acts – a couple guys from Paul Revere and the Raiders, Jimmy Griffin from Bread, Larry Henley, Dickey Lee, Bruce Channel...even Ray sang.

"Ray talked about how Elvis asked permission to record 'The Wonder of You' to which Ray said, 'You don't need my permission, you're Elvis Presley, you can do anything you want.' Elvis responded, 'Yes, I do because you're Ray Peterson.'"

Steve paused, took a deep breath. "Then Ray sang 'The Wonder of You.' He sang it from his wheelchair, and it was just as good as when he recorded it.

"He died not long after that.

"Jimmy Griffin also died months after the benefit from cancer. He never told anyone he had cancer either. He felt that night was Ray's moment."

~ Last Chance Dance ~

Later that year, Steve got word from Phil Heim that his old high school, James Monroe was going to be torn down to build a new one. Steve and Phil decided to plan a final tribute to their alma mater.

"I got the Fredericksburg Jaycees to sponsor it. The deal was I would contact the bands to perform for free and all the money would go to the music department. Every time there were budget cuts, the music department was always the first to be cut so I wanted to help.

"I called all of the guys that went to JM and played in a band. Asked them if they would sing a couple songs. If they didn't have a band still, they would be in the James Monroe *All Star Band* and we backed each other. Ended up, there were forty-eight musicians in eight reunion bands that played twenty-minutes each.

"We held it in the old gym and the tickets were $10 each. Well, the gym quickly sold out. We planned to film it, so we decided to set up a big screen in the auditorium and sold tickets there.

"The auditorium sold out. So, we decided to use the parking lot. Offered tailgate spots. Sold out there as well.

"It was a huge success. I'm not sure how much we raised but it was a lot, thousands of dollars!"

Leon Frazier also remembered that evening. "We practiced hard for the *Last Chance Dance* at James Monroe and Ronny Baker was as good as he'd ever been."

~ Back to the Beach ~

On July 29, 2007, Steve returned to Fairview Beach for a *Back to the Beach* benefit to raise money for the Fairview Beach Erosion project to repair damage from hurricanes and prevent further damage. Steve and other artists from the '60s and '70s that got their start performing at the *Starlight Pavilion* now called *Tim's II* participated.

"It rained before the end of the show, but we raised enough money to build a jetty to save the beach.

"The day before, I remember getting a call to be Taylor Swift's opening act at a show she was doing in Fairview Beach, but I was too busy with the benefit and passed on it."

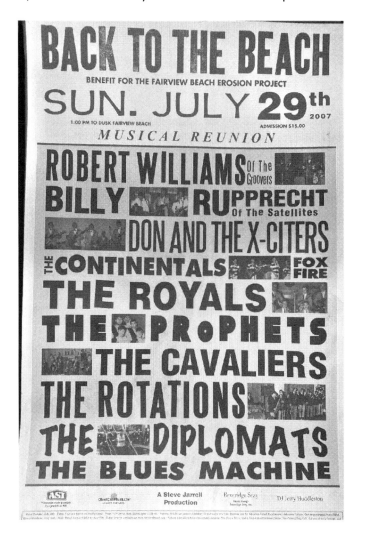

~ Sonny Geraci ~

"Dennis Tufano of The Buckinghams and I met when I worked with K-Tel in the 70's and I did the background for his recording. We remained friends.

"I'm also friends with Gary Baker, a concert promoter for the Princess Theater in Harriman, Tennessee. I was driving to play a gig in Knoxville and Gary Baker called. He was putting together an event and doing some sound checks and said, "I have someone here that says hi." Gary put Dennis Tufano on the phone.

"What are you doing," Dennis asked. "I'm in town for Gary's event and I wondered if you had time to do backup for me."

"Since Harriman was on the way home from Knoxville, I got there in time to change my shirt and play backup."

In 2013 Dennis called again to say he was putting together a benefit for Sonny Geraci who had suffered a brain aneurysm the year before. Sonny was lead singer for The Outsiders and Climax with the hit songs "Time Won't Let me" and "Precious and Few." It ended up being a two-day benefit at the *Z-Plex at Stringz 'N Wingz* in Streetsboro, Ohio.

"Dennis Tufano, Gary Lewis of Gary Lewis and the Playboys, The Rip Cords, Ron Dante with The Archies, Frank Stallone, Billy Joe Royal, Gary DeCarlo, Joey Molland, Terry Sylvester of The Hollies, Pat Upton, Jim Gold, The Vogues, Johnny Farina and many others performed. It was a BIG and successful event.

"What's interesting about that show is they had a guitar that all of us signed and then they auctioned it off. It was donated to the Rock and Roll Hall of Fame. My name is in the Hall of Fame. That is as close as I'll ever get to being in the Hall of Fame.

"Ronn Scala is a great singer but also makes championship belts. He designed a wrestling belt to be auctioned off. I think Doug Bell with Bellevue Cadillac bought it."

Signed Guitar from the Sonny Geraci benefit that was donated to the Rock and Roll Hall of Fame. Steve's autograph is just above the pickguard.

Steve with Dennis Tufano. Steve is modeling the wrestling belt designed by Ronn Scala for Sonny Geraci benefit.

~Jimmy Lowry ~

Jimmy Lowry played for popular local bands The King Bees and The O'Kaysions in the '60s before joining The Revelations Band with Larry Miller. Jimmy's wife Sylvia was still in college at the time and performed with the group as well.

Steve met Jimmy when he was released from the Air Force because of his stepfather's health and returned to North Carolina.

Shortly after that, Jimmy became lead guitar player with Donna Fargo and was instrumental in Steve joining the group after the house fire in Richmond.

When Jimmy left Donna Fargo in 1990, he joined the Sons of the Beach and is in the beach picture from Hilton Head, South Carolina. Jimmy returned to North Carolina where he died unexpectedly in 2006.

Since 2008, Sylvia Lowry and their daughter Jennie have organized an annual Jimmy Lowry Tribute for the Surry Arts Council in support of a scholarship for a graduating student excelling in music, drama, or visual arts. Steve has participated in the benefits for over ten years. Spig Davis performed at a couple of them with Steve.

During my interview with Spig Davis, who is an ordained minister, Spig talked about one Jimmy Lowry tribute where he and Steve rode together and it rained the entire way.

"We got there, and it was still raining," Spig said. "Steve commented it was a shame to travel all that way and have the show cancel.

"I said, well, let's pray for relief. Don't you know when it was time for the show to start, the sun came out and the rain went away. Steve thought that was so cool."

Steve laughed when I mentioned this to him.

"Yeah, I didn't know my keyboard player had a direct line with the Lord!"

Jimmy Lowry's wife, Sylvia Lowry.

Jimmy Lowry's daughter, Jennie Lowry.

~GIFT ~

"Another amazing friend is Buzz Cason. Buzz has done it all. He has written songs and has hits; been backup singer for Elvis Presley and Kenny Rogers; started a recording studio. Buzz had Nashville's first rock and roll band, The Casuals, was one of the original singers with Ronny and the Daytonas with 'Little GTO' as well as sang backup with Brenda Lee and Jerry Lee Lewis. He also co-wrote 'Everlasting Love' with Mac Gayden. He was also was one of the Chipmunks on the 'Christmas Album.' In later years, he would call Sons of the Beach to back him up."

Buzz and Dickey Lee organized GIFT – Giving in Faith Together – a 501(c)(3) non-profit that helps Nashville musicians and songwriters in need, whether it be medical bills, senior living expenses, hospice care or health and emergency needs. They have a website – giftnashville.org – and a Facebook page and meet monthly for lunch with an inspirational speaker or musical entertainer.

"Buzz Cason and GIFT paid for my Dad's funeral. I had done a few benefits with Buzz by then and when my Dad died unexpectedly, I didn't have insurance money to bury him."

Steve and the Sons of the Beach will often get the call from GIFT to join other musicians, provide backup with either vocal and/or sax for artists whose bands have disbanded.

The following are musicians Steve has performed with; some he had never met until that moment.

1. Jon Bauman ("Bowzer," singer for Sha Na Na)
2. Jimmy Beaumont $ The Skyliners (vocal group)
3. Chuck Berry
4. Felix Cavaliere (lead singer for The Rascals)
5. Gary DeCarlo (lead singer for Steam)
6. Ron Dante (lead singer for The Archies)
7. Ronnie Dove
8. Joe Dowell
9. Johnny Farina (Santo & Johnny)
10. Roy Head
11. Danny Hutton (lead singer for Three Dog Night)
12. Cub Koda (lead singer for the Brownsville Station
13. Gary Lewis (lead singer for the Playboys)
14. Mike Love (The Beach Boys
15. Ronnie McDowell
16. Ian Mitchell (Bay City Rollers)
17. Chuck Negron (lead singer for Three Dog Night)
18. Mitch Ryder
19. Jimmy Sohns (lead singer for The Shadows Of Night)
20. Frank Stallone
21. The Clovers (vocal group)
22. The Shades of Blue (vocal group)
23. Billy Stewart
24. Dennis Tufano (lead singer for The Buckinghams)
25. The Vogues (vocal group
26. Mark Volman (lead singer for The Turtles)

Highlights

There have been several highlights in Steve's career that he holds dear to his heart.

On September 11, 2001, Steve and millions of other Americans were glued to the television.

"I saw the planes crash into the Twin Towers and watched it over and over all day. That night, I sat down and wrote a poem, 'Army of Angels.' I wanted people to see it."

John Wayne Edwards was also affected and painted the picture "Aftermath."

"I called John Wayne and asked if he was interested in making a print of my poem with his painting. Which we did.

"Then I showed it to Spig Davis, who said, 'why don't we put some music to it and record it.' We had to adjust it some to make the song flow, but I think it turned out good.

"Spig thought the song was better suited for a female voice and felt Melody Firestone would do a good job.

"I'd never met her but am happy with how it turned out."

~ Virginia is for Lovers~

One morning, Steve was reading the paper and saw an article about the 40th Anniversary of Virginia's slogan, "Virginia is for Lovers."

"They were going to sponsor events throughout the year, one being promoting a new state song. I found myself writing the song, 'Virginia is For Lovers' and shared it with a friend, Austin Roberts.

"Austin is from the Norfolk, Tidewater area. We met in the '60s when I was playing with the X-Citers and the Prophets and he played with his local bands. We crossed paths again when I came to Nashville and we often meet and write beach music together.

"Austin sang professionally and had two good records – 'Rocky' and 'Something Is Wrong with Me.' He's also a songwriter and has written for other artists – 'Honor Bound' for Earl Thomas Conley, '100% Chance of Rain' for Gary Morris, 'Strong Heart' for T.G. Sheppard, 'You Lie' for Reba McEntire, and 'IOU' for Lee Greenwood. He has won awards for his songs and has gold records all over his house.

"Austin and I worked on the 'Virginia Is For Lovers' song, then Austin said, 'Let's go to Virginia and record it.'

"We knew other musicians from Virginia – Bill Deal and Ammon Tharp from the Rhondels were still singing at the time. Gary US Bonds was also from Virginia but lived in New York. Ended up, Bill Deal, Ammon Tharp, Austin Roberts, Gary US Bonds, and I recorded it.

"I took it to the ad agency that handled the slogan. They had turned the project over to someone else in tourism who said, 'We have our own writers.'"

Steve learned that the radio stations were running a contest for the best state song and a man from Virginia Beach involved with music, that knew they had recorded it, said he would submit it for them.

"We were all living out of state, so I said sure. I found out later, he was printing the CD and putting it in hotels to sell. He never submitted the song. We might have had a shot at it if they had heard it. Steve Bassett and Robin Thompson's song 'Virginia Breeze' was chosen."

Steve shook his head. "Another missed opportunity."

~Have You Seen This Child? ~

Steve is an early riser and does a lot of his writing at the kitchen table.

"Do you remember getting the cards in the mail or seeing the pictures on milk cartons of the missing children? My daughter, Austin, was young at the time and one day she took the pictures around the neighborhood, knocked on doors asking, 'have you seen this child? This child is lost.'

"That simple gesture tugged at my heart and I found myself writing another song, 'Have You Seen This Child.'

"I play by ear and once again, asked Austin Roberts if he would help him with a serious song. He is a Dad too. We wrote it, recorded it and Austin Roberts sang it.

"Leon Frazier was VP of Sprint/Nextel at the time. They had partnered with John Walsh and were supporting the missing child campaign. I called Leon to tell him about it."

"Send it to me," Leon said, "I'll be travelling with John Walsh this weekend to a car racing event." Leon gave it to John Walsh who gave it to Marita Rodriquez with the missing children organization.

"They liked the song and were looking for a country music star to be the spokesperson. We tried to find someone to sing it but didn't have much luck. Dolly Parton liked the song, but said her plate was full.

"I still have the song to this day."

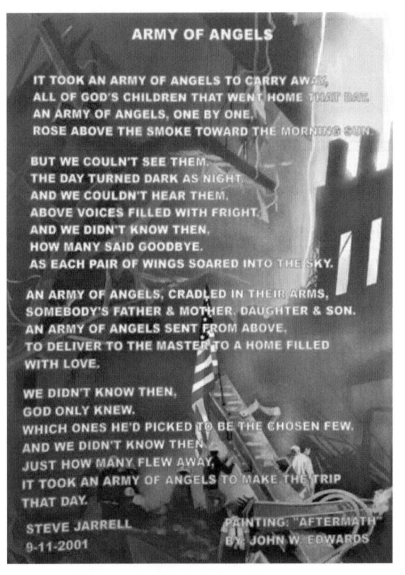

Print of Steve's "Army of Angels" poem on John Wayne Edwards' painting "Aftermath."

Virginia is For Lovers

Chorus
Virginia, is for Lovers, God must have planned it that way.
Virginia, is for Lovers, once you've been one time you'll want to stay.
No place else can give you the feeling that you can get when your right in home,
In Virginia, Virginia,…Virginia is for Lovers.

Verse1
For lovers of the mountains…the Blude Ridge can't be beat.
For lovers of the ocean…we'll put sand beneath your feet.
There's no place to step back in time
Where nothing ever seems to change.
And cities busy every night,
You'll never be the same.

Verse 2
The changing of our seasons…the moonlight on the bay.
Are just a few more reasons…to make you wanna come our way.
There's so much to see and do… you won't know where to start.
And for those who just might fall in love...this place will touch your heart,
Yes it will, oh yeah…

Bridge
There is nothing that's too far away
Always something if you want to play…

Instrumental
Refrain
Oh no place else can give you the feeling
That you can get when you're right at home
In Virginia, Virginia, Virginia is for lovers
Repeat Chorus 2X with vamp and fade

Written by Steve Jarrell and Austin Roberts
Publishers: Jarrell Music (BMI), Austin Roberts Music (SESAC)

Kay Brooks
Have you seen this Child?

I remember when she disappeared; the whole town was in shock.
She used to smile and wave at me, from her yard just down the block.
People searching everywhere, calling out her name,
Her folks prayed she'd come home again, but she never came.
(Chorus)
Have you seen this child?
She's been gone for quite a while.
Where do they go...somebody knows.
Has anyone seen this child?
Have you seen this child?

He would ride his new bike everywhere; they found it at the park.
No one even missed the boy, til it was after dark.
Ten years old so full of life, he had on his Dodgers' cap.
They heard that someone saw a van, but nothing after that.
(Chorus)
Have you seen this child?
She's been gone for quite a while.
Where do they go...somebody knows.
Has anyone seen this child?
Have you seen this child?

-Bridge-
How can a father or a mother,
Steal away their son or daughter
Knowing how much
It would hurt the other

Inst. Solo
Those pictures of the missing, I used to disregard.
Now I hear a voice say 'Daddy," and I look at every card.
(Chorus)
Have you seen this child?
She's been gone for quite a while.
Where do they go...somebody knows.
Has anyone seen this child?
Have you seen this child?

Written by Steve Jarrell/Jarrell Music, BMI and
Austin Roberts/Austin Roberts Music, SESAC

Stars & Memories

When Steve met Andy Griffith, he was filming a TV special in Nashville and in a bad mood.

"He had a bad back and wasn't interested in signing autographs or posing for pictures. I knew Andy was from Mt. Airy, N.C. because my Uncle Jimmy Childress, who owned a radio station there went to school with Andy and was friends with him.

"I took a chance and said, 'You don't know me but I'm Jimmy Childress' nephew.'"

Andy looked at Steve and said, "I'll take a picture with you."

Steve and Andy Griffith on the set of Andy's TV special.

Steve and Clifford Curry at the Carolina Beach Music Awards.

Clifford Curry had a big collection of beach records and lived in Nashville. When Steve did the show at the Ryman and tours on the road, Clifford was on all of them. Steve would often get him to close the shows with "She Shot a Hole in my Soul."

"People loved him, especially my kids – they called him Uncle Cliff. Clifford asked me to do a duet with him – Two Soul Brothers/ Just Drifting Along. When he died and they did a tribute to him at the Beach Music Awards Show. I went down and did a power point with pictures of him on the screen, took my voice off the master tape with his voice.

Clifford Curry and Steve singing "Two Soul Brothers."

"When I was on mybnr.com, Keith Angstadt was a big Johnny Mathis fan and always had two special days devoted to him — Johnny's birthday and Valentine's Day. Johnny did a show in Richmond at the Altria Theater and graciously invited the entire radio staff to come down to the show and visit backstage afterwards. The thing that impressed me most about Johnny Mathis was that at his age, he is in great health, sings as good as he ever did and is one of the nicest performers I have ever met.

Steve and Johnny Mathis at Altria Theater in Richmond, Virginia.

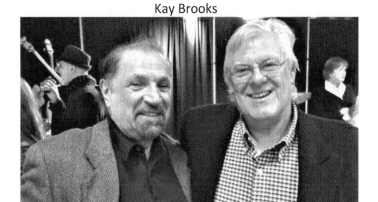

Steve and Felix Cavaliere (The Rascals) in Cleveland, Ohio after performing at a Sally Beauty Products Convention. Steve reminded the event planner that Felix would need congas for his songs for which Felix was most appreciative.

Eddie Floyd and Steve at the Beach Music Awards Show in Myrtle Beach. Eddie Floyd co-wrote "Knock on Wood" and many other songs with Steve Cropper and performed with the Blues Brothers.

Steve Cropper, Angel Cropper, Steve and Nigel Olsson.

"I have been friends with Steve Cropper for many years. We met a college in Virginia in 1968 when I was playing with The Rotations and we were the opening act when he was with Booker T. & the M.G.'s. He co-wrote 'Knock on Wood' with Eddie Floyd, 'In the Midnight Hour' with Wilson Pickett and 'Sittin' on The Dock of the Bay' with Otis Redding. Steve was also a member of the Blues Brothers Band.

"I re-connected with Steve when his wife, Angel, invited the Sons of the Beach to play for his 50th birthday party. As he listened to us perform, Steve realized we could play a whole set of his songs. He often calls me to back him up for some of his shows. He also participated in some of our benefits.

"When I was at the Alabama Theater, the *House of Blues,* located next door, was preparing for their Grand Opening. Steve called, invited me to come. Said the Blues Brothers and James Brown would be performing that evening. Since I had my own show at the Alabama Theater and would be unable to attend, Steve said 'come on over for some lunch after our soundcheck.' Steve introduced me to Jim Belushi, Dan

Ackroyd, Eddie Floyd and the other guys in Blues Brothers Band. Said I should come by after my show.

"When I returned that evening, the security stopped me from going to the private lounge upstairs. Said my name wasn't on the list. Jeff "Skunk" Baxter who played with the Doobie Brothers walked up and said, 'he's with us.'

"I went upstairs and there were all these stars. This was before cell phones, but I had bought one of those disposable cameras that were popular at the time.

"Eddie Floyd gave me a commemorative bottle of champagne and when I took my picture with James Brown, he said, 'put the bottle down. You don't want your grandkids to see it.' My biggest regret is that that camera jammed on the first picture with James Brown and none of the pictures I took that night developed!

"A few years later, Nigel Olsson, Elton John's drummer was doing a TNN National Network show interviewing players and backup musicians. The TNN people were aware I knew Steve Cropper and asked if I would introduce Nigel to Steve at his house to sort of break the ice when they did the interview.

"In 2010, Steve Cropper was inducted into the Musicians Hall of Fame in Nashville and after the induction ceremony, they had a reception party. All the STAX recording artists started jamming together with the MUSCLE SHOALS musicians and I watched from the front row. They started singing Delbert McClinton's 'Standing on Shaky Ground.' One of the guys started off the chorus but when they got to the verse, nobody knew the words! Steve Cropper motioned for me to come on stage to sing it because he knew I knew the song. I ended up being their singer for the rest of the night!

"I gave Steve Cropper a ride home that night and realized I had his amplifier in the trunk of my car. Steve said 'don't worry, I'll get it later' so I kept it in my garage for two weeks. That amplifier is now in the Smithsonian.

Steve Cropper and Steve Jarrell performing in Lexington, Kentucky.

Steve and Michael McDonald performing at Kaia Jergenson benefit in Nashville, 2000.

Steve and George Jones sharing a bite of George Jones sausages at a food trade show in Birmingham, Alabama.

Steve and Leon Frazier are the surviving members of The Prophets. They remain good friends today; talk frequently and occasionally perform together. "Leon is a great songwriter and wrote all the original songs for the Prophets. Here we are talking about recording more of his songs in the future. We'll keep you posted."

Virginia Music Hall of Fame Museum

"Around 2005, Larry Silver, a friend who is a real estate developer in Fredericksburg asked if I knew how many people from Virginia were nationally known in the music business. I began researching it, discovered a lot of names and decided our state needed a Music Hall of Fame to recognize them. I registered the name and put together a Board of Directors.

"Then Larry called to say John Elkington, owner of Performa Entertainment Real Estate was going to purchase eighteen acres at the *Celebrate Virginia* site in the *Central Park* development outside the city of Fredericksburg to build an indoor and outdoor concert facility and restaurant.

"Elkington was also going to build the museum and lease it to us for $1 per year. At the eleventh hour, the deal went down the tubes.

"I tried to keep the Board of Directors going but many have passed since then. In 2019, thanks to Lt. General Ron Christmas (Past President with the Marine Corps Museum) who is now the Chairman of the Board, Tommy Mitchell another Fredericksburg developer, attorney Aileen Heim, Kathleen Chichester (designer for the Holocaust Memorial interior), and Dr. Gregg Kimball, historian at the Library of Virginia we revitalized the Board and became an active non-profit.

"Then COVID hit and once again things have stalled.

"My goal, or legacy is to get this Virginia Music Hall of Fame established.

"There are so many – Patsy Cline, Pearl Baily, Ella Fitzgerald, Keely Smith, Wayne Newton, Kate Smith, Roy Clark, Dave Matthews, Bruce Hornsby, Robert Cray, The Statler Brothers, Gene Vincent, Ruth Brown – to name a few.

I have already contacted many of them and they, or their families are interested in sharing their memorabilia with the Museum.

"I want to leave something educational for people to visit and enjoy. Hopefully, it will happen in my lifetime.

Forever Friends

Steve, Nicky Seay and John Faulkner.

Steve, Barry Sullivan and Bill "Hook" Kain.

Nicky Seay, Robert Chinn, Steve and Kenny Whitescarver.

Bill Deal (Bill Deal & Rhondells) and Steve

Closing

"Over the years, I put on a little weight and in 2009 I travelled to Huntington, West Virginia to have laparoscopic surgery. My stomach went from the shape of a lima bean to a banana and I can only hold about six to eight ounces of food at a time. The surgery was successful and I've managed to keep the weight off."

After the divorce, Steve moved back to Fredericksburg for a brief time. "This was when I started working for mybnr.com."

He and Lee Quisenberry performed as the Sons of the Beach II at Shannon's Lounge – in the Old Sheraton – every Wednesday evening. He also performed at other clubs in the city but the music business in Virginia was not as active as in Nashville.

"So, I decided to move to Myrtle Beach where I had always played since the '70s but was always working. I figured it was time for an extended vacation at the beach. My friend and band leader Don Ballard from the X-Citers had semi-retired to North Myrtle Beach. He worked at *Graham Golf Carts* and persuaded the General Manager, Mike Graham, to give me a job in charge of their golf cart rental department. After all, living in Myrtle Beach isn't cheap and I needed a job if I wanted to stay there.

"I performed with a Sons of the Beach Duo there and had the opportunity to hear and see a lot of my peers perform. Didn't realize it would be so much fun working with a bunch of great guys. I drove the golf carts around the beach all day and managed to perform every now and then with The Embers and Jim Quick and the Coastline Band and other groups, what could be better?

"I also found Pastor Mike Lawing and his *OD Church of the Lost and Found*. You know, how I usually find somebody in the music business wherever I go? Pastor Mike used to be the promotion man for Motown Records. I always understand his messages and where he is coming from. I watch his service every Sunday morning. Good stuff.

"I was also missing my kids. After six months, I decided I had to leave. The kids were in Nashville. I had a band in Nashville. So, I went back to Tennessee where music is a business and people inspire me. I continue to write to this day."

Steve settled in Ridgetop, Tennessee.

"I like this little town. It's the highest point in Middle Tennessee. and in the old days, before air conditioning, people would buy houses and stay here in the summer— Doris Day, Willie Nelson, Grandpa Jones and String Bean.

"Then COVID hit and it was like the world shut down. I was really bored. I called Keith Angstadt with mybnr.com, asked if it was possible to go on the air a couple hours a day to help people take their minds off the virus. He said 'sure,' then built me a computer and shipped it to me in Nashville. I set up a studio in the basement and did a *Daddy-O on the Patio* show Monday through Friday, from Noon to two for a couple months.

In October 2020 Steve resumed his Daddy-O on Patio show on mybnr.com on Saturdays, Noon to three eastern time.

"Some years ago, I recorded 'Tropical Vacation.'"

He chuckled. "It's about taking a vacation in the back yard. I never released it but with all this COVID stuff, I thought the timing was right with everyone staying at home. I wanted to lighten things up, so I posted it on Facebook and YouTube. Got some good reviews. A couple radio stations around here have played it.

"I still have the Sons of the Beach but with COVID, the full bands aren't back to performing yet. In June of this year, Ken Posey and I started back as Sons of the Beach II on Friday nights."

Steve rested his head on the back in his chair, stared at the ceiling.

"You know, I've worked with the Sons of Beach since 1981.That's almost forty years," he looked at me in amazement. "And if you include my younger years and The Prophets, 2022 will make it sixty years for me in music." He laughed. "I hope I live that long!

"Seriously, a lot of my success has been about being in the right place at the right time. It hasn't always been easy. Sometimes when I was on the road, I would look at houses and be envious of families sitting at home watching TV together. There were times when I would study the newspapers just to see what city we were in.

"I loved my family, missed out on a lot but you know, survival was a priority. I followed my passion and made a lot of mistakes. If I had to do it again, I would probably concentrate on spending more time with my family and getting a college education.

"But I have really been blessed to have so many good friends! Most of my male friends from high school are still close to this day. And they always have my back.

"I guess I'd like to give a shoutout to Billy 'Hook' Kain, Robert Chinn, Paul Bruening, Barry Sullivan, John Faulkner, Nicky Seay, Fitz Johnson, Kenny Whitescarver, Larry Silver, Bootsie Howard, Rob Spratt, Corky Coble, Jimmy Franklin and Charles Weimer. Also, Hal Revercomb, John Wayne Edwards, Carey Leitch and Tom Waite who back me up whenever I perform in Virginia. I'm sure I'm forgetting someone.

"And of course, all the fans and band members I have had to honor to work with over the years. I've learned something from each and every one of them. Without them, not only the guys but the girls, I would not have had the encouragement to pursue and many times, continue in my career in music."

"What's in the future?" I asked.

"Good question. Back in the Prophets days, my dear friend Malone Schooler, told me something that I will never forget as long as I live. Malone passed in 2019 but I can still hear him in my mind.

"Stevie," he'd say, "we're in a game where we forget the losses and exaggerate the wins."

"And that's been so true with my life. There have been good times. There have been great times. And there have been down times. But God has given me the talent to continue for over seventy years and I think that my reason on Earth is to try to make people happy. My family has supported me through all of this and made several sacrifices through the years. My friends have stood by me, supported me, and given me the will to keep on doing what I'm doing. I want to keep on performing as long as I am able."

Steve performing with his Sax. Painted by John Wayne Edwards.

I've Still Got Sand In My Shoes

Written by Steve Jarrell, Jarrell Music Publishing, BMI

I used to walk along the shore, but I can't do that anymore,
And what I feel inside of me, is a longing for the sea.

I've still got sand in my shoes and some rhythm and blues
to remind me of where I'm from.
The Tams and Rhondels and those sweet southern belles
singing all of my favorite songs...I've still got sand in my shoes.

My friends hear me talk about that old boardwalk,
And they all think that I'm insane.
But they ain't never done a good shag dance,
and they don't know the words to the songs I sing.

I've still got sand in my shoes and some rhythm and blues
to remind me of where I'm from.
The Tams and Rhondels and those sweet southern belles
singing all of my favorite songs...I've still got sand in my shoes.

Maybe I can go back one of these days.
And feel that salty mist hit my face.
And watch the waves while they kiss the sand,
While walking with my baby hand in hand.

I've still got sand in my shoes And some rhythm and blues
To remind me of where I'm from.
The Tams and Rhondels And those sweet southern belles
Singing all of my favorite songs...I've still got sand in my shoes.

Carolina Man

Written by Steve Jarrell, Jarrell Music Publishing, BMI

Wore out my weejuns at the American Legion last night.
Ruined my docksiders wading in the water, in the early
morning light.
And you say that you don't like to shag,
"Hey Baby" just ain't your bag.
Well it don't bother me cause I'm Carolina Man. (Yes I am)

I gotta rip in my khakis, it may be tacky. Who cares about
that?
I got button down collars and only two-dollars, but that'll buy
me a beer.
And you say that you don't like to shag,
"Hey Baby" just ain't your bag.
Well it don't bother me cause I'm Carolina Man. (Carolina
Man)

Well you say you like the boys from Harvard and Yale.
They ain't no good for you honey I can tell.
And the California boys from UCLA,
They don't worry me cause they're too far away!

I got some jack in my pocket and I'm flying like a rocket. (clean
out of sight)
Swingin' and a swayin' to beach music player, feels so right.
So baby come along with me.
If you don't I'm gonna set you free,
Cause I'm a high preppin', fast steppin', cool breezin', no
reason, finger poppin', no stoppin', Carolina Man.

And I'm telling you Ma'am yes I am, a Carolina Man.
And I'm telling you Ma'am yes I am, a Carolina Man.

Southern Belle

Southern Belle, can I ring you sometime?
Might as well, spend my last dime.
You look so fine, walking in the sand...I wanna call you if I can
Mm...my Southern Belle

Maybe tomorrow if you've got nothing to do,
We'll go down to the ocean just me and you.
We'll build castles, write our names in the sand,
I wanna be your loving man,
Mm...My Southern Belle

When you turned and smiled at me I was swept away,
Like a shell from the sea in the Chesapeake Bay.

Southern Bell, I know you're kind of shy,
Cause you won't even look me in the eye.
I've tried so hard to make you notice me,
Baby don't you see, I love you
My Southern Belle

When you turned and smiled at me, I was swept away,
Like a shell from the sea in the Chesapeake Bay.

Southern Belle, won't you take a chance with me.
Southern Belle, that's the way it ought to be.
You look so fine, walking in the sand.
I want to hold you if I can, be your loving man.
Mm...my Southern Belle
My Southern Belle
My Southern Belle

DISCOGRAPHY

SINGLES

I STILL LOVE YOU	THE PROPHETS	SHELL	1965
BABY	THE PROPHETS	SHELL	1965
FIGHTIN' FOR SAM	THE PROPHETS	STONEL	1966
MISTY	THE PROPHETS	STONEL	1966
I'LL KEEP DRIFTING & DREAMING	THE PROPHETS	LOOK	1967
ALL OF MY LIFE	THE PROPHETS	LOOK	1967
LOOKING AT YOU FROM A DISTANCE	THE PROPHETS	REUNION	1978
FEELINGS ARE JUST MEMORIES	THE PROPHETS	REUNION	1978
LINDA	SALT AND PEPPER	HEATWAVE	1969
A MAN OF MY WORD	SALT AND PEPPER	HEATWAVE 1969	
MR. MAGIC MAN	OUR HOUSE	SANLEE	1983
UP ON THE ROOF	OUR HOUSE	SANLEE	1983
CAROLINA MAN	SONS OF THE BEACH	SILVERS	1987
PERSONALITY	SONS OF THE BEACH	SILVERS	1987
I'VE STILL GOT SAND IN MY SHOES	SONS OF THE BEACH	RIPETE	1989
COUPE DE VILLE	SONS OF THE BEACH	RIPETE	1990
TIL NEXT SUMMER	SONS OF THE BEACH	RIPETE	1990
TWO SOUL BROTHERS	W/CLIFFORD CURRY	GRAND STRAND	1993
JUST DRIFTIN' ALONG	W/CLIFFORD CURRY	GRAND STRAND	1993
A MAN OF MY WORD	SALT AND PEPPER	KENT (U.K. LABEL)	2009

ALBUMS

SIGNED D.C. (COMPILATION)	THE PROPHETS	SATAN	1984
CAYMAN VACATION	SONS OF THE BEACH	AUSTIN	1986
PARTY IN PARADISE	SONS OF THE BEACH	SILVERS	1987

CD COMPILATIONS

BILL DEAL & AMMON THARP - THE ORIGINAL RHONDELS
VIRGINIA IS FOR LOVERS S. JARRELL, B. DEAL, A. THARP, A. ROBERTS, G. BONDS

NEW OLDIES AND ORIGINAL BEACH MUSIC
STILL KICKIN STEVE JARRELL & THE SONS OF THE BEACH

SWOOP DOWN JESUS 2
THIS LITTLE LIGHT OF MINE   STEVE JARRELL AND GREG ROWLES

BOOGIE TIME – ROCKIN' THE ROOTS
COUPE DE VILLE   STEVE JARRELL & THE SONS OF THE BEACH

BE YOUNG, BE FOOLISH, BE HAPPY AGAIN
I'VE STILL GOT SAND IN MY SHOES   STEVE JARRELL & THE SONS OF THE BEACH
SOUTHERN BELLE   STEVE JARRELL & THE SONS OF THE BEACH
CAROLINA MAN   STEVE JARRELL & THE SONS OF THE BEACH

DIGITAL RELEASE

FRIENDS	STEVE JARRELL	2018

FILMOGRAPHY

MOVIES:

TITLES:	CLIENT:	CASTING:	DIRECTOR:
MY BODY, MY CHILD (Vanessa Redgrave)	ABC Movie of the Week	featured extra	Marvin Chomsky
SWEET DREAMS (Jessica Lange, Ed Harris)	Tri-Star Pictures	featured extra	Karel Reisz
ERNEST GOES TO JAIL		extra	
THE THING CALLED LOVE	Paramount Pictures	extra	Peter Bogdanovich
A BLUE DENIM ROSE		Principal	unknown
THE STUEY UNGAR STORY (Michael Imperioli)		extra	A.W. Vidmer
ACQUITTED BY FAITH (Casper Van Dien)	Brad Allen	extra	Daniel Lusko
THE MESSIAH (Michelle Monaghan, Mehdi Dehl)	Netflix	extra	Mark Burnett

TELEVISION:

HAWAII 5-0 (Jack Lord)			
LET'S GO ROCK N ROLL	Viacom	co-host	Deanna Deck
NIGHT OWL THEATRE	WKRN	host	WKRN
ELVIRA, MISTRESS OF THE NIGHT	WZTV	principal	WZTV
MUSIC STREET (TV Pilot)	L.A. Connection	co-star	Eric Straton
NASHVILLE NOW	TNN	guest/performance	TNN
NOON SHOW	WSMV	guest/performance	WSMV
RONNIE MILSAP-LOST IN THE 50'S (special)	TNN	guest/performance	TNN
GATLIN BROS.-GREAT GATLIN GETAWAY	TNN	guest/performance	TNN
BEACH BOYS-BRING ON THE SUMMER (special)		performance	Network special
ROCK N ROLL GRAFFITI	Gabriel Communications	music director	PBS special
700 CLUB - TODD AYER STORY	CNB	principal	CBN
NASHVILLE (C. Britton, C. Esten, H.Panettiere)	CMT	extra (4episodes)	Callie Khouri

MUSIC VIDEOS:

HEY BARTENDER (JOHNNY LEE)	CMT	co-star	Dean Daniels
YOU REALLY GOT A HOLD ON ME (M. GILLEY	CMT	principal	Dean Daniels
ANOTHER DRINKING SONG (JOHNNY NAIL)	CMT	principal	Dean Daniels
SO GOOD (THRASHER BROTHERS)	CMT co-star	D	ean Daniels
WARNING SIGNS (BILL ENGVALL)		principal	
BLUE MOON OF KENTUCKY (JESSICA LANGE)	Thorn-EMI/MCA	co-star	Karel Reisz
POP A TOP AGAIN (ALAN JACKSON)		principal	

COMMERCIALS:

PICKERS' SUPPLY (regional)	AVS Communications	lead	
SERVICE MERCHANDISE (national)	Thom II Productions	principal	
PURVIS FORD (regional)	WFLS Fredericksburg, VA	lead	
DUKES OF HAZZARD (regional)	WTVF-TV	lead	WTVF-TV
4-THE LOVE OF SUMMER	WSMV-TV	lead	WSMV-TV
BRIDGESTONE (national)		principal	

Backup Band

Steve Jarrell and the Sons of the Beach have backed many recording artists in concert. To the best of his recollection, the following is a listing of those artists:

1. Jewel Akens
2. Len Barry
3. Archie Bell (lead singer for the Drells)
4. Bonnie Bramlett (Delany & Bonnie)
5. T. Graham Brown
6. Buzz Cason (recording name Garry Miles)
7. Bruce Channel
8. Jimmy Clanton
9. Dee Clark
10. Earl Thomas Conley
11. Helen Cornelius
12. Steve Cropper (guitar player for Booker T. & MGs, Blues Brothers)
13. Clifford Curry
14. Bill Deal
15. Carl Dobkins Jr.
16. Frankie Ford
17. Carl Gardner (lead singer for the Coasters)
18. Danny & the Juniors (vocal group)
19. Ian Gillan (lead singer for Deep Purple)
20. Dobie Gray
21. Jimmy Gilmer (lead singer for the Fireballs)
22. Jimmy Griffin (Bread)
23. Henry Gross
24. Jimmy Hall (lead singer for Wet Willie)
25. The Happenings (vocal group)
26. Richie Havens
27. Gladys Horton (lead singer for the Marvelettes)
28. Larry Henley (lead singer for the Newbeats)
29. Gene Hughes (lead singer for the Casinos)
30. Con Hunley
31. Brian Hyland
32. Jimmy "Handyman" Jones
33. Robert Knight
34. Denny Laine (lead singer for the Moody Blues, guitar player for Paul McCartney & Wings)
35. Dickie Lee
36. Barbara Lewis

37. Jerry Lee Lewis
38. Ketty Lester
39. Michael McDonald
40. Bret Michaels (lead singer for Poison)
41. Jerry Naylor (lead vocalist for the Crickets after Buddy Holly's death)
42. Leroy Parnell
43. Ray Peterson
44. Sandy Posey
45. Jay Proctor (lead singer for Jay & the Techniques)
46. Johnny Preston
47. Larry Raspberry (lead singer for The Gentrys)
48. Jimmy Rodgers
49. Tommy Roe
50. Dave & Sugar (vocal group)
51. Nedra Ross (the Ronettes)
52. Billy Joe Royal
53. Merrilee Rush
54. Dee Dee Sharp
55. Troy Shondell
56. Melanie Sifka (Melanie)
57. Dave Somerville (lead singer for The Diamonds)
58. Joanie Sommers
59. Joe Stampley
60. Dodie Stevens
61. Billy Swan
62. Gary Talley (The Boxtops)
63. Fingers Taylor
64. Johnny Tillotson
65. Pat Upton (lead singer for Spiral Starecase)
66. Freddy Weller (Paul Revere & the Raiders)
67. Dottie West
68. Bucky Wilkin (lead singer for Ronny & the Daytonas)
69. Maurice Williams (lead singer for the Zodiacs)
70. Otis Williams (lead singer for the Charms)
71. Al Wilson
72. Mary Wilson (the Supremes)
73. Dennis Yost (lead singer for the Classics IV)

Kay Brooks

Say "John Faulkner!"